Set aside any previous notions of hospi
course meal or beautifully manicured
encourage you to see tangible and everyda
to those in your sphere of influence; it wil.   ....r your eyes to see what
a gift, privilege and joy it is to reflect the hospitality of our Savior.

SARAH WALTON, Author, *Together Through the Storms*

I loved this book. I was expecting a guilt-fuelled, task-list-populating, exhaustion-inducing exhortation to be the host with the most. What I got was a heartwarming, rich and motivating conversation with Carolyn as we dug into the Bible and gloried in the gospel together. Rather than cajole you into dutiful hospitality, this book inspires you to joy-inducing, gospel-rich hospitality. The fruit will be seen in extraordinary hospitality being demonstrated across the church family to the glory of God.

JONATHAN GEMMELL, The Proclamation Trust

Extraordinary Hospitality (For Ordinary People) fueled my desire to welcome others as Christ so richly welcomes us. Carolyn Lacey winsomely challenges us to humbly sacrifice not only our homes but also our efforts, skills and time to the one who gave us his very life.

HUNTER BELESS, Journeywomen

Deeply theological and refreshingly practical, this book paints the picture of an overflowingly generous God, and seeks to help us be transformed more into his likeness. By taking a wide-angle view of hospitality, this book shows how we can all use our time, energy, home, possessions, talents and words to bless others as God has first blessed us. It is inspiring, challenging, beautifully written and full of grace.

MATT SEARLES, Author, *Tumbling Sky*

Carolyn's view is wide, as she encourages us to look beyond our friends to see those in need. Her ideas are creative—I am looking forward to inviting more people here to cook for me! But her goal is so simple: to help us love others humbly and practically, for the glory of God. How liberating!

HELEN THORNE, Biblical Counselling UK

What will inspire you to bother with hospitality? Turns out it isn't getting a new cookbook. We need instead to raise our gaze and explore the wonders of how God has welcomed us in the gospel. This thought-pro-voking book will help you do just that—and then give you lots of creative ideas on how you might begin to reflect God's "hospitality" in your own.

JULIA MARSDEN, Author, *Forgiveness*

The thought of hospitality makes some break out in hives and others start dusting off the serving dishes. Whichever you are, you will walk away from this book encouraged and convicted, and with practical insight into how to live out a life of welcome.

COURTNEY REISSIG, Author, *Teach Me to Feel*

Such a warm, challenging and encouraging book—lunch breaks, Sunday seating, washing up and dinner tables interwoven with glorious gospel truths, all pointing to the ultimate host. A very handy little book!

GABBY SAMUEL, Women's Ministry Development Worker, FIEC

Carolyn Lacey lets in the light of how wonderfully generous God is to us, and so she inspired me to be like him. If you would love to be a cheerful giver, rather than a reluctant one, then read here and in the Bible what God had in mind when he told us to "practise hospitality".

LIZ COX, Minister for Women and Community, St. Giles' Derby, UK

In this inspiring book, Christian hospitality is beautifully defined and illustrated as the practical reflection of God's generosity to us in Christ. Carolyn helps us see that it is not about perfect homes or fancy cooking but an attitude of the heart that any Christian can put into practice.

JULIAN HARDYMAN, Senior Pastor, Eden Baptist Church, Cambridge, UK

Hospitability reveals our trust and confidence in the grace of God in Christ. In this fantastic book, Carolyn Lacey covers the biblical teaching on hospitality in helpful and practical ways. It will leave you amazed at the grace of God and equipped to engage in hospitality to others.

DAVE JENKINS, Servants of Grace Ministries

A gentle and biblical encouragement to show the same generous and indiscriminate welcome to others as God shows to us. Using passages from throughout the Bible, Carolyn Lacey moves us beyond guilt-inducing images of "entertaining" to a gospel-focused, other-centred ministry of love.

CLARE HEATH-WHYTE, Author, *Old Wives' Tales*

A warm and insightful book on a vital biblical theme. We worship an amazingly generous God, and as we practise hospitality, we reflect his character. In this pastorally sensitive and biblically balanced book, Carolyn Lacey anticipates and answers many of the questions that come to mind when we think about hospitality. Soaked in Scripture and full of practical advice, this book is highly recommended.

PAUL MALLARD, Pastor, Widcombe Baptist Church, Bath, UK

CAROLYN LACEY

EXTRAORDINARY HOSPITALITY

(for ordinary people)

thegoodbook
COMPANY

Published by:
The Good Book Company

thegoodbook.com | thegoodbook.co.uk
thegoodbook.com.au | thegoodbook.co.nz | thegoodbook.co.in

The author photograph was taken by Megan Cobbett.

ISBN: 9781784985745 | JOB-007579 | Printed in the UK

Design by André Parker

For Andy and Kath:
You reflect God's generous welcome in so many ways.
It has been my privilege to learn from you.

Carolyn Lacey is a writer, speaker, pastor's wife and mother to two teenage children. Based in Worcester, UK, she teaches the Bible regularly at women's events and conferences.

CONTENTS

FOREWORD

This fresh and lively book, full of grace, earthed in reality, soaked in Scripture, has prompted me to reflect that it is more blessed to give than to receive.

It is most certainly a blessing to receive hospitality. I think of my early—and tiring, and rather lonely—days as an unmarried schoolteacher in my twenties in a small town far from home, and the kind older couple who repeatedly welcomed me to their home for Sunday lunch. I think I often stayed much longer in the afternoon than they might have wished, but they never let me know if that is how they were feeling! I think of countless friends who have refreshed my and my wife Carolyn's hearts with their kindness, opening their homes to us again and again. What a blessing to be on the receiving end of such open-hearted kindness!

And yet the Lord was right: it is more blessed to give than to receive (Acts 20 v 35). Such hospitality as we have been able to offer has reflected far more on my lovely wife's kindness than on mine. But what a blessing it has been, and continues to be, to welcome others into our home and our lives. What riches of relationships, and often of enduring friendships, have been experienced and nurtured in those contexts! Friends' letters or emails are often sweetened with happy memories of time spent together—and the blessing they brought to us, which far exceeded anything we may have been able to do for them.

One of the many features of this book I have appreciated is the imaginative flexibility with which Carolyn Lacey enters into the very different circumstances to which the call to hospitality may come. Since getting married 38 years ago, my experience has perhaps been stereotypical for a man of my generation—a wife who loves to host, a succession of homes in which to live, and sufficient income to share. But this book recognises so many other contexts: those without homes suitable for welcoming others, men and women with inadequate income, and so on. Whoever you are, whatever your state of life, there will be something here for you.

Some of us brighten up at the mere mention of hospitality; it puts a light in our eyes. *Tell me more, give me ideas, I love this.* Others may groan inwardly, feeling that perhaps we ought to read this book, but wondering if we really have to. Wonderfully, there is something here—and perhaps some happy surprises—for you, whoever you are and however you feel about these things.

I write this during the coronavirus lockdown in the UK. I have been thinking that these days of being barred from welcoming others into our homes may have provoked one of four responses.

Those who just love to be hospitable to a rich variety of people found lockdown deeply distressing; they longed for the unlocking that would enable them to go back to cheerful and vigorous hospitality. How good if that is you. How healthy to grieve at "social distancing," however necessary it may have been for a period.

Quite a few of us had grown a little weary of the costliness of hospitality, perhaps discouraged at how little evident fruit we saw from our investments into people's lives. If we are honest, we may have to admit that we loved the quietness and relished being able to have no one else in our homes, while keeping a joyfully clear conscience because the government forbade it! For many, lockdown was—in some measure—a blessed time of sabbath. If that is so, I pray that this sabbath will issue in renewed gladness and zeal in showing hospitality as and when we are allowed to do so again.

Perhaps for some this was a time quietly to pray, review, and make godly resolutions for imaginative and creative ways of pouring out the kindness and welcome of God to others. If that is you, this book could be just God's timely provision: those are exactly the things which it will help you with.

But I suppose some must face the fact that lockdown didn't really change how many people came into their homes, or how often, because they have never begun to learn the joy of hospitality. If that is you, please take this book as a most encouraging and bracing challenge to change!

May God bless you in fresh ways as you read, and grant you—like me—to feel again the truth of the Lord's words: it is more blessed to give than to receive.

Christopher Ash

AN INVITATION

"Oh no! You're not going to tell us we need to have more people round for dinner, are you?"

That was my friend Debbie's response when I told her that I was writing this book. I was surprised: Debbie is a fantastic cook, confident and outgoing, and always seems to have people staying in her home. But even she evidently feels overburdened and exhausted by the idea of hospitality.

I have felt like that too.

One low point came after a particularly long morning at church. I had arrived early to practise with the band, played for the service, had long conversations with a few people I knew were struggling, prayed with a couple of others, and was now trying—unsuccessfully—to extract my kids so we could get home. A well-meaning woman drew me aside and suggested that I think about having more people round for lunch on Sundays. She was concerned that my husband had been the pastor of our church for a couple of years and there were people we still hadn't had over. Yes, I had small children, worked part-time and was involved in several different ministries; but another local pastor's wife always had ten people over for Sunday lunch, she pointed out, while I only ever seemed to invite a few at a time. I went home feeling guilty, discouraged and exhausted. The idea of hospitality had become a burden.

A few years later, I was teaching on the New Testament qualifications for church leaders (in 1 Timothy 3 and Titus 1). As we noted that an elder must be hospitable, I found myself asking, "Does Paul really mean that his wife (if he has one) must be great at cooking for loads of people? What if he doesn't marry? What if he marries a wife who struggles with anxiety or depression—or an eating disorder? What if he suffers with those things himself? What if he lives in a tiny flat with no dining table? What if he's an introvert? What if...?"

It is not just church leaders: the Bible calls all followers of Jesus to "practise hospitality", regardless of marital status, salary or house size—and to do it "without grumbling" (Romans 12 v 13; 1 Peter 4 v 9). But nowhere does it talk about tableware or traybakes. Neither does it link hospitality with expense, exhaustion or an extroverted personality.

So I'm not going to do that either.

We will all have friends who are great at hosting people for meals in their homes. Some are confident cooks; others are confident enough to say they're not—and order in! But most of us have many *more* friends who find the idea of hospitality overwhelming. Even some of those who appear to be great at hospitality secretly struggle with it.

It's time to rethink what hospitality is all about.

I want to show that hospitality doesn't have to be exhausting and overwhelming. And that is because it is not so much about *what* we do, but *why* we do it.

This is not a "7 Steps to Becoming the Perfect Host" book. Rather, it is an invitation to join me on a journey, learning to welcome like Jesus does. You won't need a large house or a dining table that seats eight—Jesus never hosted a fancy dinner party! You won't need a big food budget or lots of free time. You won't even need to be especially outgoing or confident. You just need to delight in God's welcome and desire to reflect it to those around you.

So over the next seven chapters we will look together at seven characteristics of God's welcome and see how they should reshape our welcome. Read as slowly or as quickly as you like—on your own, with a friend or in a discussion group. It may be most helpful to read one chapter each week, taking time to reflect and pray. At the end of each chapter there are a few questions to help you.

I have made lots of practical suggestions throughout the chapters. If you try to do them all, it will be overwhelming—and that is not the point of this book! Pick just one or two practical points from each chapter and start to weave them into your daily habits. If you do, you'll be encouraged by how simple hospitality can be—and how rewarding it is too.

I imagine that, like me and like Debbie, you feel very ordinary. I don't want to persuade you otherwise—we are ordinary. But our God is extraordinary. He invites us to reflect him in ordinary places to ordinary people—and he can do extraordinary things through us as we do.

COME AND EAT
BECOMING GENEROUS

King George IV of the United Kingdom knew how to throw a dinner party. On 18 January 1817—a few years before he became king—George gave a banquet in Brighton in honour of the visiting Grand Duke Nicholas of Russia. He hired the world's best (and most expensive) chef to prepare a feast to impress, and the banquet was a great success. The chef prepared no fewer than 127 dishes—including a four-foot-high Turkish mosque made entirely of marzipan. George was so happy that he declared, "It is wonderful to be back in Brighton, where I am truly loved".

Prince George felt loved because his chef prepared exotic food and his guests were impressed with him. He thought a successful party should be marked by personal satisfaction, praise and popularity.

Are you ever tempted to think like this too? It is natural to be easily impressed with extravagance, and we all love receiving praise. So we can fall into the trap of believing that our hospitality should look like George's—just on a smaller scale. The house must be perfect, the conversation sparkling, the food delicious.

If you're like me, that makes hospitality seem like a burden rather than a joy. I'm busy, I don't have lots of spare cash, I'm tired most of the time—and I'm not that great with marzipan! However much I like the idea of putting on a lavish banquet, it's just not realistic.

Thankfully, God doesn't ask or expect this of me.

Instead he simply calls me to reflect him in the way I relate to others. As a follower of Jesus, I am being transformed into his image (2 Corinthians 3 v 18). Most people don't connect holiness with hospitality—I didn't until recently. But becoming like Jesus means welcoming as he does.

Here's the simple truth: God is generous, so we should be generous too. We can't compare ourselves to God— he is incomparable in every way. But as we reflect on his extraordinary generosity in welcoming us, we will find ourselves wanting to become more generous in the way we welcome others.

Isaiah 55 gives us one of my favourite pictures of God's cheerful, big-hearted, open-handed, ungrudging, freely given, forever-satisfying welcome:

> *"Come, all you who are thirsty,*
> *come to the waters;*
> *and you who have no money,*
> *come, buy and eat!*
> *Come, buy wine and milk*

without money and without cost.
Why spend money on what is not bread,
 and your labour on what does not satisfy?
Listen, listen to me, and eat what is good,
 and you will delight in the richest of fare.
Give ear and come to me;
 listen, that you may live.
I will make an everlasting covenant with you,
 my faithful love promised to David.
See, I have made him a witness to the peoples,
 a ruler and commander of the peoples.
Surely you will summon nations you know not,
 and nations you do not know will come running
 to you,
because of the LORD your God,
 the Holy One of Israel,
 for he has endowed you with splendour."

Seek the LORD while he may be found;
 call on him while he is near.
Let the wicked forsake their ways
 and the unrighteous their thoughts.
Let them turn to the LORD, and he will have mercy
on them,
 and to our God, for he will freely pardon.

 (Isaiah 55 v 1-7)

THE GREATEST HOST

Do you ever wonder if God is really interested in you? If he really wants to be close to you? These verses show the deep, heartfelt desire of God to be close to his people.

In verses 1-3 he calls out not once but five times: *Come! Come to me!*

These words were spoken to people living in exile. God's people, Israel, had forsaken him. They had run after other gods and, because of their sin, God had handed them over to their enemies. He had given them what they most desired: friendship with his enemies and freedom from the laws which were designed for their good. And yet, in these verses, his extravagant, lavish love overflows into an animated call to come back to him.

God is not a reluctant host. His invitation isn't motivated by duty or obligation. No, he is delighted to welcome! There is a building sense of excitement, longing and intensity in his invitation as he calls out, *COME! COME! PLEASE COME!* He is joyful and enthusiastic in his welcome. And, unlike so many hosts, he expects nothing in return.

> *You who have no money,*
> *come, buy and eat!*
> *Come, buy wine and milk*
> *without money and without cost. (v 1)*

God offers a free invitation to all; no one is excluded, because there is enough for everyone. He will meet every need. The thirsty will drink; the hungry will eat well. He will provide for those who cannot provide for themselves— no strings attached! Those who have known the famine of exile will be introduced to the abundant provision of the promised land: milk, wine and "the richest of fare". This will be a generous, lavish feast. It will be good and satisfying, delighting everyone who will come and eat (v 2).

And, although the guests have nothing to offer in return, this isn't merely a charitable handout. It is not the equivalent of a free meal at the local soup kitchen but a permanent seat at the royal table. God delights to share all he has with his people. He is the ultimate "cheerful giver" (2 Corinthians 9 v 7)!

This is a picture of what God has done for us. Like Israel, we had turned our backs on him, but in Christ he has welcomed us back into a relationship with himself. He has provided for our needs—offering us forgiveness for sin and life that lasts for ever. We are able to become part of his family.

It might sound like a contradiction to invite people to "buy ... without money", but God wants us to know that the things that usually come with a cost—such as wine and milk—are free for us to enjoy. There is a great cost to be paid for this lavish feast—but it is not paid by the guests. The payment required for the wine and milk of the feast in Isaiah 55 has been made by the suffering Servant described two chapters earlier: Jesus.

After he has suffered,
he will see the light of life and be satisfied;
by his knowledge my righteous servant will justify many,
and he will bear their iniquities. (Isaiah 53 v 11)

We are welcome at God's feast because of Jesus. He has paid with his life so we can be made right in God's sight and acceptable to him. He has covered the cost. All we need to do is accept the invitation. That is what God's generous hospitality looks like.

NO LONGER GRUDGING

When I think of generosity, I think of my friend Neil—the most generous person I know. He loves to share his home, his time and his gifts, and he is joyfully sacrificial with his money. When his first wife died, one of the first things Neil did was buy a slow-cooker—so that he could continue to invite friends, neighbours and church family to join him and his two boys for meals, despite his busy workload and increased family responsibilities. He has eyes for the needy and works hard to relieve burdens and show care. I have benefitted from his generosity in more ways than I can count.

Yet most of us are not like Neil. So often our hospitality fails to reflect God's cheerful generosity. If I'm honest, my heart can be reluctant or resentful even when I am offering what looks like generous hospitality. Inviting others into my home—and into my life—often feels inconvenient. I don't naturally want to share my food, my time or my energy with others. I am a grudging giver rather than a cheerful one. Perhaps you feel like this too.

The problem is our hearts. God wants his people to be generous and open-handed, but our hearts often get in the way.

Deuteronomy 15 helps us see the connection between our hearts and our hands. As Moses unpacks the law, he tells the Israelites how they are to treat those who have less than they do:

> *If anyone is poor among your fellow Israelites in any of the towns of the land that the LORD your God is giving you, do not be hard-hearted or tight-fisted*

> *towards them. Rather, be open-handed and freely lend*
> *them whatever they need ... Give generously to them*
> *and do so without a grudging heart; then because of*
> *this the LORD your God will bless you in all your work*
> *and in everything you put your hand to.*
>
> *(Deuteronomy 15 v 7-8, 10)*

Our hearts control our generosity. Those with hard hearts will be tight-fisted towards their neighbours; those with soft hearts will be open-handed. This applies to Christians in the context of our hospitality. Like the Israelites, we have been rescued from slavery and redeemed at great cost. God has poured his grace and mercy into our lives. He has given us what we don't deserve and could never earn—forgiveness, acceptance, assurance of eternal welcome. And as our hearts are softened by his extravagant generosity towards us, we will delight to be like him by being open-handed towards others. We will want to share our time, our money, our possessions and our homes—not grudgingly but generously (v 10).

Our love for the Giver will overspill into generous love for others.

A CHANGE OF HEART

This is not something we can achieve by ourselves. If we want to offer hospitality that is open-handed and generous, we need God to change our hearts. But how will this happen? Around 700 years after Isaiah's prophecy, Jesus stood in the temple courts of Jerusalem and repeated the invitation:

Let anyone who is thirsty come to me and drink.
Whoever believes in me, as Scripture has said, rivers
of living water will flow from within them.
(John 7 v 37-38)

This "living water" is the Spirit, who is given to those who believe in him (v 39). This means that, as believers in Jesus, we have his Spirit living in us. And it is his Spirit that can transform our hard hearts so that we can love and welcome others as he does. If, like me, you sometimes struggle to welcome others into your life, God's Spirit has the power to change your feelings and motives. He is able to equip you with both the desire and the ability to offer a generous welcome to those he has put in your life.

Jesus offers grace to us, but he also offers grace to others through us. He promises that living water will flow from within us to others—that is, he will extend his welcome to others through us. This is the best motivation for offering generous hospitality. Generosity is not just something we are called to do—an item to tick on the spirituality checklist. It is a significant way in which God works in our lives to bring life to others.

THE VERY BEST

So what will it look like to make generous hospitality part of everyday life? How can we show genuine, generous welcome without becoming exhausted and overburdened?

We need to start by rejecting the world's picture of superficial hospitality. Our goal is not to show off our homes or our cooking skills (or lack of them!) but our Saviour.

This takes a bit of humility—and we will think more about that in chapter 3. But while our unbelieving friends or work colleagues may use their homes, their money, and their abilities to impress, we want to use ours to bless.

At the same time, we will also want to give our best when we can. Isaiah 55 shows that God's feast is generous and lavish. The thirsty need water, but God offers milk and wine. He gives much more than the bare minimum. And you and I should do the same. With the Spirit's help, we should be enthusiastically open-handed and generous with all we have.

In my previous church there was an older widowed lady named May, who regularly invited students to her home for Sunday lunch. She didn't have much money but chose to eat simply during the week so that she could afford to buy meat for a roast on Sunday. Her friend (another widow) provided the dessert. The students would enjoy a home-cooked meal and then fall asleep on May's comfy sofas while she cleared up. May told me once that she had never been much of a cook when she was married but decided to practise after her husband died so that she could offer somewhere that felt like home to the students. She wanted to use what she had been given to benefit others.

You only become like this when you understand that all you have has been given to you by God so that you might glorify him with it. Anyone who believes that their home and possessions are theirs to use for their own pleasure will not want to share. But when we realise that God gives us good gifts so that we can use them to benefit others, we are liberated to share them joyfully.

We also need to think about who God wants us to give our best to. It can be tempting to try to impress those who already have a lot while making less of an effort for those who don't expect much anyway. But the gospel reshapes our hospitality. It calls us to be most generous to those who are most in need—those who cannot offer anything in return. This is how we reflect God's generosity towards us.

YOU CAN DO IT!

The invitation to join God in offering generous hospitality is not restricted to those who are wealthy or have large houses. The goal of hospitality is to reflect God's welcome, and we can all do that, regardless of our bank balance or living situation. If you live in a shared space or have a limited food budget you may find it difficult to invite people home for meals regularly. But there are plenty of ways to be generous. You could pull up a chair and eat your lunch alongside someone who is on their own, for example. You could be generous with your time by introducing yourself to a new neighbour or work colleague and offering to show them around or help them get settled. Regardless of our finances, we can welcome others into our lives by being generous with whatever we have.

Here is a list of a few types of gifts that God gives us. Look over it now and try to think creatively about how you could use each of these gifts in ways that will reflect the extraordinary welcome of our generous God—and point your friends and neighbours, both Christians and non-Christians, to him.

- Your time
- Your energy
- Your home
- Your possessions
- Your creative talents
- Your practical skills
- Your words

In fact, it is worth pausing to think over these things regularly. Generosity will require a bit of planning. Try looking at your diary or calendar at the beginning of each week. See if there is a small window of time you could share with someone who is in need of company or encouragement. Then make a call or send a text to arrange something—and do this straight away, because if you leave it for another time the window will disappear. Other things will crowd in and your good intentions will be forgotten, or you'll feel too overwhelmed to follow through with them.

While hospitality doesn't have to involve food, we do all need to eat every day, so sharing a meal can be an opportunity to express friendship and welcome that is also time-efficient. Most of us eat two or three meals every day. That's between 14 and 21 meals every week— not including cups of tea and coffee. To share just one or two of those meals with someone else is not all that costly in terms of time or energy, but it could massively impact those whom we invite into our everyday living.

I mentioned my friend Neil earlier. Jason is someone who has been impacted by Neil's hospitality in this way. Jason suffers with various physical disabilities and learning difficulties, which make it hard for him to engage socially, either in the local community or at church. A couple of years ago, Neil's church organised a weekend of prayer. The idea was that people would gather in each other's homes at mealtimes to eat and pray together. Neil realised that Jason could easily feel excluded from this weekend: he wasn't used to being in other people's homes and would struggle with being in a big group. So he invited Jason to join him and his boys for a quiet family breakfast—along with a woman named Sarah who also has learning difficulties and is unable to speak. The five of them shared breakfast together; then Neil and the boys read and prayed through a short psalm while Jason and Sarah listened.

Sharing breakfast and a psalm was an easy thing for Neil and his boys to do, but it was a significant morning for Jason. He realised that he was welcome and wanted— in Neil's home as well as in the church—and that he could feel comfortable sharing life in this way. He joined the family for breakfast again a while later and, shortly after that, agreed to try out the small-group Bible study that meets in Neil's home. He has been an active part of that small group ever since.

Who could you invite to share a meal with you next week? Is there someone at work you could invite out for a coffee on the way home? Or a neighbour you could invite in for a bowl of soup or a pizza (shop-bought is fine!) on the weekend? Is there someone in your church small group who rushes home after work but still struggles to cook, eat and get to the group on time? Could you suggest they come straight to your house on their way home to share a quick meal before going to the Bible study together? These are only small changes to your everyday routines and habits of eating and drinking—but they are big opportunities to welcome the people God brings into your life. And they are a chance for those people to experience for themselves what God is like: how generous, kind and full of love he is.

TRUE SATISFACTION

As we think about practical ways to show generous welcome, we need to remember the purpose. In Isaiah 55, God's invitation is not for a one-time banquet but to eternal life.

> *Seek the LORD while he may be found;*
>   *call on him while he is near.*
> *Let the wicked forsake their ways*
>   *and the unrighteous their thoughts.*
> *Let them turn to the LORD, and he will have mercy*
> *on them,*
>   *and to our God, for he will freely pardon. (v 6-7)*

The goal of God's hospitality is a restored relationship with him. We want to join him in calling our friends, neighbours and church family to the feast of mercy and forgiveness. This is the only feast that is truly satisfying and life-giving. We must not be content to offer superficial hospitality that looks good but does nothing to satisfy the deepest longing of the human heart—to know and enjoy our Creator.

> *Why spend money on what is not bread,*
>   *and your labour on what does not satisfy? (v 2)*

Superficial hospitality, like that of George IV, can only provide temporary satisfaction. If you were invited to the most extravagant feast imaginable—marzipan mosques and all—and you ate all you possibly could, you would only be full for a short while. Before long you would be hungry and need to eat again.

As Christians, the supreme goal of our hospitality should be to offer what will truly satisfy. This doesn't mean we shouldn't share meals—eating together is a great way to communicate welcome and cultivate friendship. But we want to offer more than just food and drink. We want to point others to the cheerful, big-hearted, open-handed, ungrudging, freely given, forever-satisfying welcome of our God. Our reward is the joy of leading some to him for the first time, of strengthening others who are disheartened, of being encouraged and uplifted ourselves, and of delighting in him together.

Verse 5 of Isaiah 55 speaks of the blessing that will come to other nations as Israel returns to God:

> *Nations you do not know will come running to you,*
> *because of the LORD your God,*
> *the Holy One of Israel,*
> *for he has endowed you with splendour.*

The special relationship between God and his people will attract others to "come" too. This is what we hope for as we offer a generous, open-handed welcome. It is possible for our hospitality to reflect God's and showcase the relationship we have with him. This means using every opportunity we have to speak about his generous invitation to life, whether we are reminding one another or giving a first hint to unbelieving friends. Ultimately we will be pointing to God as the greatest host—the one who will give living water. We are calling out with Jesus, "Come!"

QUESTIONS FOR REFLECTION

Read Isaiah 55 v 1-7 again. What do you find most appealing here? What picture of God is presented?

In what specific areas do you struggle to be a generous giver? Why do you think that is? What lies are you believing? What truths are you forgetting?

How will this picture of God's welcome reshape your hospitality?

WHO IS MY NEIGHBOUR?
BECOMING COMPASSIONATE

Who is your favourite "love-to-hate" character? Mine is Mrs Jellyby from Charles Dickens' novel *Bleak House*. Mrs Jellyby is a compassion-faker. She's obsessed with her latest social project—the relocation of poor families to Africa, where they will improve life for the Borrioboola-Gha tribe. But while Mrs Jellyby spends every waking hour campaigning for her Borrioboola-Gha venture, her own children run wild—dirty and uneducated. Her husband is neglected and left bankrupt by her project. And the homeless children sweeping the streets around the Jellyby home are invisible to her. She is passionate about the needs of the far-off Borrioboola, but blind to the needs of the people in front of her.

I'm sure Mrs Jellyby would describe herself as compassionate—after all, she spends her life working to help those less privileged than her. But her activity is not really motivated by compassion. When her Africa project fails (the King of Borrioboola sells everyone who survives the change of climate for rum!), Mrs Jellyby moves quickly on to another cause. She loves her projects more than the people they are designed to help.

I dislike Mrs Jellyby but, if I'm honest, I also see myself in her. I like the idea of being a compassionate person, but I don't always find it easy to show genuine compassion to those around me—or even to feel it. If you're like me, you'll find yourself more naturally drawn towards comfortable hospitality—that is, hospitality which focuses on people who are easy to spend time with, who don't demand too much and whose circumstances you can relate to. We may like the idea of being part of a church family that welcomes people with messy lives, but we don't always want to get involved in the mess ourselves. We want our churches to be places where the marginalised and vulnerable find a home, but we don't necessarily want the responsibility of speaking or working on their behalf.

But God's hospitality isn't comfortable and convenient. It is compassionate.

COMPASSION OVER CONVENIENCE

In Luke 10, Jesus tells a story which highlights what true compassion looks like.

The story is introduced when an expert in Jewish law asks Jesus how he can gain eternal life. It seems like a reasonable question, but the lawyer is testing Jesus. He knows that the law says that he must love God with all his heart, soul, mind and strength, and love his neighbour as himself—that is how to gain eternal life. The problem is that he doesn't obey it fully; he doesn't love others as much as he loves himself. So, to justify his lack of love, he asks, *Who is my neighbour? Who is it I'm called to love as myself?*

It is the wrong question. The lawyer wants Jesus to tell him who he must love, and he wants an excuse for not loving others in the same way. He may as well have asked, *Who do I not have to love? Who is excluded from this commandment? The Romans? The tax collectors?*

Jesus shows why this is the wrong question to ask by telling the story of the good Samaritan. This is a familiar story for most of us, but we mustn't let familiarity blind us to its significant challenge.

> *Jesus said: "A man was going down from Jerusalem to Jericho, when he was attacked by robbers. They stripped him of his clothes, beat him and went away, leaving him half-dead. A priest happened to be going down the same road, and when he saw the man, he passed by on the other side. So too, a Levite, when he came to the place and saw him, passed by on the other side."*
> *(Luke 10 v 30-32)*

The priest probably reasoned that if the man was already dead and he touched the corpse, he would become "unclean" according to God's law (Leviticus 21 v 11). That would mean being unable to fulfil his priestly duties. So he walked away. The Levite was also among the religious elite—someone who worked at the temple, cleaning sacred objects, looking after money and performing music for temple worship. He, too, saw the dying man and passed by on the opposite side of the road. The shock to the original hearers is this: two men who should have been among the most compassionate both prioritised their own convenience.

When we hear this story, most of us judge the priest and the Levite. They knew God had commanded them to "Love your neighbour as yourself," and they failed to obey. But can we honestly say that we wouldn't fail in exactly the same way? We all know how easy it is to ignore need—to pretend we haven't noticed the neighbour struggling to start their car or the person who always sits alone at church. We all understand the temptation to walk on the other side of the street and hope someone else will stop to help.

Of course, the greatest twist in the story is not the response of the first two men but the identity of the third: a Samaritan.

The Samaritans were long-standing enemies of the Jews. The hatred between Jews and Samaritans went back centuries—all the way to the time of the exile. The Samaritans had been Israelites who intermarried with their Assyrian captors and built a rival temple for their own worship. In Jewish eyes, they were now unclean outsiders. It's hard to fully express the level of animosity between the Jews and Samaritans—we could maybe compare it to the hostility between Israel and Palestine today. But Jesus introduces the Samaritan as the hero of the story.

But a Samaritan, as he travelled, came where the man was; and when he saw him, he took pity on him. (v 33)

The Samaritan, like the priest and the Levite, has reasons to avoid the Jewish man by the side of the road. But when he sees him, he feels compassion for him. He bandages his wounds and takes him to an inn to care for him. The Samaritan's compassion is genuine. It makes him willing to enter into the man's suffering—even though this is costly and inconvenient. He pays generously for the man's ongoing care (two silver coins was enough for several weeks' food) and promises to return and cover any additional expense.

When Jesus follows up his story by asking, "Which of these three do you think was a neighbour to the man who fell into the hands of robbers?" the answer is obvious. The man's enemy proved to be his neighbour. The priest and the Levite knew what the law said—they would have recited part of it that morning. But the Samaritan was the one who put it into practice.

Only those who love God with all their heart, soul, mind and strength will love their neighbour as themselves. This is what the lawyer needs to understand. He may think he is doing his duty towards God by studying and teaching the Scriptures, but his love only goes so far. He doesn't love God with all his heart. Jesus tells him, "Go and do likewise" (v 37). In other words, *You go and love your enemies too. Yes, even the Romans and the tax collectors.* To us he might have said, *Even the difficult neighbour, the depressed colleague, the newcomer with rudimentary English, the older acquaintance with unsavoury political views.*

Go and do likewise.

DIFFERENT QUESTIONS

The question from the lawyer which prompted this famous parable assumes that there are some people who are his neighbours and others who are not. This enables him to put boundaries around his compassion—he will love his neighbours but not his non-neighbours. We can be like this too. We ask, "Who must I welcome? Who must I invite into my home? Who do I have to make space for?" We may as well ask, "Who do I not need to welcome? Who am I free to overlook or ignore? Who can someone else welcome?"

But Jesus doesn't divide the world into neighbours and non-neighbours like this. His question shows that we should treat everyone as a neighbour—especially those who are most in need. He helps us ask the better questions: "Who needs my welcome? Who do I have the opportunity to show generous hospitality to? Who has God placed in my path so that I may reflect his compassion?"

These are the questions we should ask as we look around our church, our workplace and our neighbourhood. They will help us think about who God wants us to show hospitality to. They will keep us from comfortable hospitality that prioritises ease and convenience over another's need.

Two friends of mine, James and Sarah, do this really well. Every Sunday they look out for people who are new to church or a bit on the fringe, and invite them to their home—sometimes for meals, sometimes to play board games. They choose not to spend time only with friends who are like them. Instead they look out for people who struggle with loneliness, grief, anxiety, depression or difficult family circumstances. They prioritise compassion over comfort and convenience.

James and Sarah have a different perspective from that of the lawyer. He wants to inherit eternal life, but they know that they have already inherited it—not because of anything they have done for others but because of what Jesus has done for them. None of us are able to obtain eternal life by our own efforts. None of us can be this good a neighbour to every person we meet. The good news is that Jesus has been this good a neighbour to us. He was hated and rejected, but he had compassion on his enemies. When we were dying, he intervened to save our lives at the cost of his own—on the cross. He has given us the life we could never earn.

This means we don't need to do anything to inherit eternal life. If we trust in Christ, it is already guaranteed. But we must still love God with all our hearts, and we must still love our neighbour as ourselves—not as a way of earning his love but as a response to it. Jesus calls us to love others as he has loved us: selflessly, sacrificially, compassionately.

What will this look like in the context of our hospitality?

BEING A NEIGHBOUR

It is easy to feel overwhelmed by need. We are bombarded with appeals for compassion from so many places—disaster reports from overseas, local charities, mission agencies, social-media campaigns, people struggling in our own churches and communities. It's hard to know who to help, and how.

In some ways, it's easiest to focus on the far-off needs because they demand no more than cash and a signature. We can think that once we've donated to a few charities or JustGiving pages we have done our bit. Or, like Mrs Jellyby, we can convince ourselves that because we help with causes far away, we don't need to show compassion to those on our doorstep.

The needs closer to home can feel more burdensome. We fear the physical and emotional cost of getting involved in other people's struggles. The thought of entering into suffering and need can be overwhelming. When you allow yourself to become weighed down by worries about this person or that person, it can leave you feeling crippled—unable to respond to anyone at all. Or, if you're not careful, it can lead to indifference. You might try to shut out need as a strategy for coping, or you may become so used to witnessing suffering that you are no longer moved by it. No one wants to fall into that trap, but the alternative seems to be burnout.

How can we avoid both these pitfalls? How can we seek to offer genuine, compassionate welcome to those who most need it, without becoming overwhelmed or burnt-out?

Here are four suggestions.

Pray

As Christians, we believe that God sovereignly ordains every part of our lives—that includes our address. He places us in homes, neighbourhoods and church families so that we might reflect his love and compassion to the people around us. But he doesn't leave us to figure out how to do this on our own. If you're struggling to know who needs welcome, ask him to make it clear.

Walk or drive around your neighbourhood. As you do, ask God to open your eyes to your neighbours' needs. Ask for specific opportunities to show compassion. Think about what that might look like. It could be something practical like providing meals, offering lifts, looking after pets, arranging appointments, or helping with jobs. Or it could be something as simple as asking about someone's day, listening to their worries, giving a hug.

Next Sunday, look around your church family (or, if you can't get to church, look through your membership list or prayer directory). Who is most in need of your compassion? Who is lonely or grieving? Who struggles with depression or anxiety? Who is caring for a disabled family member? Who seems unhappy, distracted or stressed? Ask God to help you show welcome and care.

Pray for opportunities to offer welcome to those who are rejected, marginalised or persecuted because of their faith in Jesus. It is increasingly likely that there will be believers in our church communities who experience hostility from their families and friends as they hold to biblical viewpoints that are considered hateful or harmful. We need to be family to these individuals. Ask God to prepare you for your part in that.

Avoid favouritism

While considering who to welcome, we need to be careful not to focus our efforts only on people we find easy. When you look around your church family, ask yourself: "Who is unlikely to receive a phone call or text or dinner invitation this week?" That is probably the person God wants you to care for.

It is not that we shouldn't make time for our friends or family. And it is not wrong to build relationships with people who share our interests or who are at a similar age and stage of life as us. But we mustn't focus all our attention here. Throughout the Bible, God emphasises the need for his people to care for the poor, vulnerable and needy. James is especially clear in his letter that favouritism is inconsistent with love for God. He warns his readers against favouring the wealthy, and he reminds them that true religion involves caring for the vulnerable:

> *Religion that God our Father accepts as pure and faultless is this: to look after orphans and widows in their distress and to keep oneself from being polluted by the world.*

> *My brothers and sisters, believers in our glorious Lord Jesus Christ must not show favouritism. Suppose a man comes into your meeting wearing a gold ring and fine clothes, and a poor man in filthy old clothes also comes in. If you show special attention to the man wearing fine clothes and say, "Here's a good seat for you," but say to the poor man, "You stand there" or "Sit on the floor by my feet," have you not discriminated among yourselves and become judges with evil thoughts? (James 1 v 27 – 2 v 4)*

Choosing to welcome some types of people and not others—whether that's because of wealth and social status, as in James' example, or for any other reason—is putting ourselves in God's place as judge. But believing in Jesus Christ means accepting *his* verdict about people. The parable of the good Samaritan reminds us of God's compassionate care towards us when we were his enemies. He has favoured the underserving and unlovable, and he wants us to do the same.

Accept the cost

Compassion compels us to share the weight of another person's burdens, and this is never easy. It means being willing to sacrifice comfort and convenience. This is unnatural for us. We are hard-wired to love ourselves more than others. But Jesus tells us to love others as we love ourselves; this is the measure of our love for God. What will help us as we wrestle with our reluctance to show compassionate welcome to others? We need to look to the cross.

The cross is the measure of God's compassion for us. It reminds us that true compassion means being willing to enter into another person's suffering. It means identifying a need and working to relieve that need—despite the cost. The cost may be to our weekly food budget or our clean carpets as we open our homes to welcome individuals and families who need a place of refuge. It may be to our time or energy as we look for opportunities to serve others in practical ways. And it may be to our reputations as we advocate for those whose dignity is threatened—the poor, those who are disabled, refugees, victims of trafficking or the homeless.

We need to be realistic about the cost of compassionate hospitality, but we don't need to fear it. We can be confident that God will provide all we need—physical strength, emotional energy, time, money, patience and grace.

Depend on grace

My family enjoys watching Marvel films. There's something compelling about a "save the day" story. We love to see our favourite superheroes enter into problems of injustice, conflict and suffering, and bring peace and resolution.

I like the idea of playing superhero to my neighbours who are in need. I want to swoop in with my special ability to solve problems—and then move on. I fear I won't have the stamina for longer-term relationships with people who are unlike me and might need so much from me. I'm aware that my patience is limited, my physical strength is weak and my emotional capacity is low. I feel I lack the resources to enter fully into my neighbour's suffering. Perhaps you do too. At these times, we need to remember that we are not called to be the chief burden-bearer—Jesus is.

Come to me, all you who are weary and burdened, and I will give you rest. (Matthew 11 v 28)

Rather than retreat in fear, we can move towards our needy neighbours in dependent faith on God's power to equip and sustain us. We may not have all the resources we need, but he does. We can initiate a compassionate welcome, confident that God will provide all we need. We can depend on his grace to sustain us in relationships that feel difficult or demanding. We can trust that the

One who has been a neighbour to us will equip us to be a neighbour to others.

A century ago, the poet Annie Johnson Flint wrote about her dependence on God's inexhaustible supply of grace to sustain her through a life of intense physical suffering. Her words can encourage us when we feel too weak to offer compassionate welcome.

> *His love has no limit, his grace has no measure,*
> *His power has no boundary known unto men.*
> *For out of his infinite riches in Jesus,*
> *He giveth, and giveth, and giveth again.*

SEEING WITH GOD'S EYES

My husband and I visited Beirut in the summer of 2002. Twelve years after the end of the Lebanese civil war, Syrian soldiers continued to occupy the bullet-marked streets of the city, intimidating and threatening its residents. Today, many Lebanese regard Syrians with resentment and distrust, and the presence of Syrian refugees has been overwhelming—emotionally as well as physically. But, despite this history of resentment and conflict, the church in Lebanon is embracing Jesus' command to be a neighbour to those who were once enemies. They provide food, blankets and practical care for Syrian families in tent settlements; run education centres for refugee children; offer counselling for adults; and extend hospitality, friendship and acceptance.

Resurrection Church in Beirut has worked hard to welcome and care for Syrian refugees since they started to arrive in 2011. Now, 70 percent of the congregation are refugees. Preaching on Psalm 23 one Sunday, Pastor Hikmat Kashouh told them, "You are most precious. The Shepherd gave his life for you. You are the guest of honour at a feast that never ends."

If we are to become more compassionate in our hospitality, we need to look at the people around us through God's eyes. We need to see our neighbours as God sees us—as flawed image-bearers in need of mercy and kindness. No one has to "deserve" our compassion. No one is unlovable. Like the lawyer who came to Jesus, we need to understand that loving God means loving the people he loves.

C.S. Lewis wrote in *The Weight of Glory*:

> *"There are no ordinary people. You have never talked to a mere mortal ... it is immortals whom we joke with, work with, marry, snub, and exploit— immortal horrors or everlasting splendours."*

Remembering that everyone we meet is eternal should transform the way we view our neighbours. Their souls will last into eternity—either in eternal glory or eternal suffering. If we want our neighbours to know glory, we must be willing to make opportunities to point them to God's eternal welcome. This will be costly and inconvenient. But this is how Jesus has loved us—and this is how he calls us to love others.

Go and do likewise. (Luke 10 v 37)

Who do you find difficult to love? Who most needs your compassion? Will you be a neighbour?

QUESTIONS FOR REFLECTION

Reread the story of the good Samaritan and think about how Jesus has been a neighbour to you. What is your response to his compassion?

Who are the people you find most difficult to be a neighbour to? How will remembering how Jesus has been a neighbour to you help you in your welcome of them?

Look back through the practical ideas in this chapter (in the section "Being a Neighbour"). What one specific thing will you do this week to show a compassionate welcome to someone who needs it?

DIRTY FEET

BECOMING HUMBLE

Supper is ready. The candlelit room is fragrant with the aroma of herbs, spices, roast lamb and freshly baked bread. The friends, dressed in white, take their places on mats arranged like a horseshoe around the low table, eager to begin the feast. Wine is poured as they lean in, ready to share their food and tell their stories.

As the meal is served, Jesus pushes himself up from his mat, takes off his cloak and wraps a towel around his waist. He pours water into a basin and begins to work his way around the group of friends, washing the dust and dung from their feet and drying them with his towel.

The atmosphere changes as excited conversation is replaced by embarrassed silence.

Foot-washing was a familiar feature of hospitality in the ancient Near East. When guests arrived at a home, their sandal-clad feet dirty from the dusty streets, a slave would wash their feet. Here, Jesus reverses the roles. Instead of taking his rightful place as the honoured guest, he takes on the role of the lowest servant.

It was just before the Passover Festival. Jesus knew that the hour had come for him to leave this world and go to the Father. Having loved his own who were in the world, he loved them to the end. (John 13 v 1)

Jesus knows that it is the last evening of his earthly life. He knows he will soon die an agonising and shameful death. But his mind is not focused only on his suffering—he is also thinking about his friends. He is about to save the world, yet he picks up a towel to wash his disciples' dirty feet. Jesus will show his love in the greatest way imaginable: on the cross. The foot-washing is the precursor to that. It is an act of humble, self-sacrificing service that provides an example for the disciples—and us—to follow.

Jesus also knows which of his friends will betray him (v 11). We might expect him to confront Judas and expose him as a traitor in front of the other disciples. But Jesus doesn't wield knowledge and power as a weapon. Rather, he embraces a humble posture and washes feet that will later run from him in fear, denial, betrayal.

Humility characterised Jesus' earthly life and ministry. Born to parents who could not afford a lamb for a burnt offering (Luke 2 v 24; Leviticus 12 v 6, 8), he never used his power or position as the Son of God to his own advantage. At this point he has spent the last three years of his life teaching his disciples about the upside-down nature of the kingdom of heaven—the last will be first and the first will be last—but they still don't understand. They are uncomfortable with humility. That is why Peter says, "You shall never wash my feet" (John 13 v 8).

TWO KINDS OF PRIDE

We are uncomfortable with humility, too. We can find it hard to accept acts of humble service ourselves; and at the same time, we can also struggle to serve others. The problem is our pride—our tendency to think more of ourselves than we should.

Pride hinders our hospitality in two ways. On one hand, it keeps us from reaching out to the people most in need of our welcome because we think that we are somehow above them. On the other hand, it inhibits us from welcoming others because we worry about what people may think of us. These obstacles to hospitality may look very different, but they are two sides of the same coin.

The first of these forms of pride is the most obvious. Our Western culture encourages self-promotion rather than self-sacrifice. It tells us to strive for position, popularity and praise. It pushes us to demand respect and honour from others rather than to give it to them. And we are easily persuaded! Our hearts are naturally inclined towards self rather than others, so this way of thinking appeals to our innate desire for glory. We tell ourselves that we are entitled to keep and enjoy what we have—our money, our homes, our food, our free time. We worked for them, we deserve them, and we shouldn't have to share—especially not with people who we think are less deserving than us.

But in chapter 2 we saw there is no one we are not called to love and serve. Rather than thinking too highly of ourselves, we need to remember that we are the needy, unlovable ones whom Jesus has stooped to serve.

The second form of pride is more subtle. It is at the heart of many of our fears associated with welcoming others:

They will see what I'm really like, and they might not like me.

They will see what a mess my home is and how bad my parenting skills are—and then they won't respect me.

I can't do it as well as others. I'm not a great cook.

I find it difficult to make conversation—I'm not funny or interesting or articulate.

I might offend the people I don't invite.

I may be criticised for inviting the "wrong" people.

These fears arise when our view of others is too big. They are symptoms of a greater fear which the Bible calls the "fear of man" (Proverbs 29 v 25). But at its heart lies our desire for approval. This is another form of pride—of putting ourselves first. We want people to think well of us. Fear of others is one of the greatest obstacles to open-handed, compassionate hospitality. Welcoming people into our lives makes us vulnerable to disapproval, disappointment and discouragement. If our fear of what people think of us is greater than our love for them, we will be reluctant to offer welcome.

When we hold back from showing hospitality—either out of selfishness or out of fear—we show that our view of self is too high. We need a new perspective: a bigger view of God.

Meditating on God's greatness, power and splendour brings our view of self into perspective. Remembering that our purpose is to bring him honour and glory frees us from an unhealthy preoccupation with our own image or reputation. It liberates us to serve others humbly.

Jesus serves his disciples from a position of greatness:

> *Jesus knew that the Father had put all things under his power, and that he had come from God and was returning to God. (John 13 v 3)*

Knowledge of his high position enables Jesus to adopt a low position. He knows that becoming a servant will not weaken his status as God the Son. He doesn't need to be served by others, because there is nothing he needs; everything belongs to him. Jesus has all authority, honour and glory, and he serves willingly from this high position.

We can have the same attitude because if we are in Christ, our identity comes from him. When we are tempted to think of ourselves too highly, we should remember that we are weak, sinful and undeserving, but that God has given us new life in Christ. When we are tempted to fear what other people think of us, we should remember that God has exalted us with Jesus (Ephesians 2 v 6). This high position in Christ frees us to serve others humbly and joyfully. We can be confident that by humbling ourselves and serving as Jesus did, we lose nothing of this eternal status.

Joshua Abraham Norton was a nobody until September 1859, when he marched into the offices of the San Francisco Bulletin and proclaimed himself "Emperor of these United States". Previously unknown—and bankrupted by a number of unsuccessful investments and lawsuits—Norton had decided he was the answer to the country's flawed political and legal systems. Dressed in a military suit and feathered hat, and carrying a ceremonial sabre, "Emperor Norton I" paraded the streets of San Francisco for 21 years—inspecting buildings, cable cars and police uniforms.

Of course, despite his ambitious claims, Joshua Norton had no real status or significance. He was an ordinary man with an extraordinary sense of self-importance. He had no good reason to expect honour from his fellow citizens, but he demanded it anyway. Unlike Jesus—who, despite his high position, was willing to humble himself and serve—Norton lived for his own undeserved praise and glory.

We might laugh at Norton's eccentricity. It is incredible that he got away with such ridiculous behaviour. But his presumption stemmed ultimately from pride: he thought a lot more of himself than he should have. And when we are proud—when we put ourselves first instead of Jesus and then others—we have a view of ourselves that is just as disproportionate as Norton's. And just as ridiculous. God is the most important person in the universe, not you or I.

GOING TO WAR

To humbly submit to God's authority has been humanity's greatest struggle since life in the garden. Ever since Adam and Eve sided with the serpent, humans have fought for self-rule, self-sufficiency, self-promotion, self-satisfaction and self-glory. And even though as Christians we are new creations in Christ, these deep-rooted tendencies continue to surface—especially when we think about serving others.

To engage in Jesus-shaped hospitality is to go to war against our pride. It means choosing to embrace humility. It means valuing others above ourselves, seeking others' interests above our own and becoming like Christ in our attitude to others (Philippians 2 v 3-5). No wonder it's hard! But Jesus calls us to follow his example.

When he had finished washing their feet, he put on his clothes and returned to his place.

"Do you understand what I have done for you?" he asked them. "You call me 'Teacher' and 'Lord', and rightly so, for that is what I am. Now that I, your Lord and Teacher, have washed your feet, you also should wash one another's feet. I have set you an example that you should do as I have done for you. Very truly I tell you, no servant is greater than his master, nor is a messenger greater than the one who sent him."
(John 13 v 12-16)

Jesus is saying, *If I am willing to serve you, you can have no reason not to serve one another.* If we want to follow him, we must be willing to serve like him—not primarily in extraordinary ways, but in the everyday, ordinary moments of life.

Inviting a grieving widow out for coffee might feel like a small gesture, but it could be the means God uses to lift her gaze from her loneliness and loss to his goodness and grace. Helping with childcare might not seem like a fruitful way to spend a morning, but if it enables a new mum to join a Bible-study group, where she can learn from God's word and grow in faith, it's invaluable. Driving a minibus full of boisterous kids to a youth-group camp may not feel significant or fulfilling, but it may result in one of them understanding the gospel for the first time and turning to Christ for salvation.

American satirist P.J. O'Rourke writes in his book *All the Trouble in the World*, "Everybody wants to save the Earth; nobody wants to help Mom do the dishes." He has a point. It's easy to want to reflect Jesus in his greatness; but Jesus served in mundane as well as magnificent ways. You and I live most of life in the mundane: momentous occasions are few and far between. So we need to be content to serve in the mundane—in ways that are unnoticed, uncelebrated and unglamorous. We need to look for ways to reflect Jesus in his humility. We need to ask: what could be our equivalent of washing feet?

DOING THE DISHES IN ALL OF LIFE

Hospitality is a tangible way of demonstrating humility because it involves putting others before ourselves. It is a way of communicating to someone else that they are significant, that their needs matter to us, that we value them. And, like foot-washing, hospitality requires no special talent or skill—just a humble, selfless, other-centredness.

In the home

Inviting people into your home can feel risky: you are putting yourself, your possessions and your relationships on display. But if you avoid giving in to your craving for approval or fear of disapproval, you can do this cheerfully. Remember that the goal is to bless, not to impress. Here are some things to remember about humble hospitality in the home.

First, don't be overly anxious about clearing everything away before guests arrive. While it is nice to provide somewhere comfortable and relaxing to sit, the house doesn't need to be spotless—no one relaxes in a show-home! God has given us our homes not to function as high-end hotels for the elite and privileged but to serve as places of respite for the weak and weary. The weak need encouragement, comfort, and strengthening; the weary want rest. Worrying too much about what guests think of your home is a form of pride—it shows that you are more concerned about impressing people than meeting their needs.

Second, accept help. Most people will feel more comfortable if they can contribute. If you are providing a meal and someone offers to bring something, say yes. It doesn't matter that you may be able to organise everything yourself—it's far more important to show that you appreciate someone else's contribution. You don't want to give the impression of being omnicompetent—and you need to remember that you're not! Likewise, if your guests really want to clear up, let them. Mutual acts of service cultivate intimacy in our relationships.

Lastly, take time to think about what your guests need. Are they lonely, tired, hungry, stressed, celebrating, grieving? Some people like to offload at the end of a busy day; others like to sit quietly for a bit. I have a friend who enjoys playing a board game with my children while I cook—it takes her mind off work and helps her feel part of the family. Try to think about what would most encourage, refresh and nurture each person who comes to your home rather than what you would most like to do. This is an opportunity to show we value others above ourselves and care more about their interests than our own.

In the workplace

Most people don't go to work thinking about how they can serve their colleagues; but followers of Jesus are different. We know that our status, significance and security as children of God and co-heirs with Christ is unchanging, so there is no risk in looking for ways to welcome and invest in others. While our colleagues may seek to elevate themselves, we can champion others. This is what humility looks like—elevating others above ourselves. We can look for ways to affirm, encourage and celebrate someone else's efforts or achievements. We can advocate for others even if that means the loss of our own reputation or progress. This kind of love is completely unexpected to most people—just imagine how it will make them feel!

In a "time is money" environment it's easy for work colleagues to feel disconnected—like strangers inhabiting the same space. When work needs to get done, it is tempting to view people and relationships as unwelcome interruptions. Taking a break to eat lunch with a colleague or stopping to help someone with their project may mean staying later into the evening to finish your own work. But to do so is to put someone else above yourself; it is to follow Christ's example of serving others even when your own needs are pressing.

Hospitality seeks to turn strangers into friends. This will look different for each of us in our various work contexts. Think about your workplace. How could you communicate welcome and friendship to your colleagues—especially those you don't know well? Here are some suggestions:

- Let people know you don't mind being interrupted: smile, initiate conversations, and say yes to requests for help as often as you can.
- Ask others for help. Don't be afraid to say you don't know something or can't do something by yourself; let your colleagues know that you need and value their input.
- Support and encourage or mentor those who have less experience than you.
- Make tea or coffee for your colleagues—don't only serve yourself.
- Be an enthusiastic participant in team-building events, inter-departmental competitions and nights out. Don't be aloof or give the impression that you don't value time with colleagues.
- Remember birthdays, religious festivals or other significant occasions—even if they're not important to you personally.
- Wash up coffee mugs, clean up shared spaces, and do other jobs no one else wants to do.

These are just suggestions—not a prescription. You'll know what is most appropriate in your context. And there is no need to feel burdened by a long list of things you ought to do; just choose one or two to begin with. The point is simply to think intentionally about how you can turn strangers into friends through humble acts of service.

In church

When we meet as a church family, it is easy to focus on our own needs and desires. But practising humble hospitality reorients us. It reminds us that we are not consumers looking to have our needs met but co-hosts with Christ. It encourages us to look for opportunities to communicate welcome by serving others. It makes us willing to do the tasks no one else wants to do—without needing to be noticed or thanked.

I'm grateful for members of my church who model this well. As I write, I'm thinking about a senior university lecturer who directs traffic in the car park patiently and cheerfully, even when it's pouring with rain; a management consultant who faithfully stacks and unstacks chairs and tables each week and works hard to make sure our meeting spaces are comfortable and accessible; a friend with a high-powered legal job I don't understand who regularly makes coffee, washes up, welcomes guests, serves communion and befriends the lonely. These friends reflect Jesus' humility. They may have a high status in the workplace, but they delight to serve others rather than being served themselves. And their acts of humble service make our Sunday gatherings accessible and welcoming, both for the church family and for newcomers.

Following Jesus' example means being willing to pursue the humble tasks rather than leaving them to someone else. And it means being willing to serve without prejudice or favouritism. Jesus served Peter and John, but he also served Judas. There should be no one—church member or guest, enemy or friend—whom we are not prepared to serve.

Pursuing humility may also mean being willing to stand back so that others have opportunities to use their gifts. We must be willing to let go of what we love—the roles or activities we are tempted to find our identity in—and take on roles that are less appealing.

UNLESS I WASH YOU…

Humble hospitality is hard, and it is often costly in our culture. So we need a compelling reason to persevere in it. Jesus gives us the motivation we need:

> *He came to Simon Peter, who said to him, "Lord, are you going to wash my feet?" Jesus replied, "You do not realise now what I am doing, but later you will understand."*
>
> *"No," said Peter, "you shall never wash my feet." Jesus answered, "Unless I wash you, you have no part with me."*
>
> *"Then, Lord," Simon Peter replied, "not just my feet but my hands and my head as well!" (John 13 v 6-11)*

Peter's initial response is interesting. He won't allow Jesus to serve him in such a menial way. At the same time, he doesn't want to be the one to serve his friends; otherwise he would take the towel and basin from Jesus and wash the other disciples' feet himself. Peter believes that greatness demands service from others. He does not realise that Jesus serves his friends not in spite of his greatness but because of it.

But Jesus is clear: only those who allow themselves to be served by him will belong to him. Once Peter understands this, he is filled with enthusiasm.

We need to understand this too. We can only belong to Jesus if we if we accept the way he has served us—on the cross. And as those who have been served, we now serve others.

I have set you an example that you should do as I have done for you. Very truly I tell you, no servant is greater than his master, nor is a messenger greater than the one who sent him. Now that you know these things, you will be blessed if you do them.
(John 13 v 15-17)

QUESTIONS FOR REFLECTION

Imagine yourself among the disciples at the last supper. How would you have responded to Jesus washing your feet? What is your response to the way he has served you on the cross?

In what ways does pride most often hinder your hospitality? What will it look like for you to "go to war" against your pride?

In which context—home, work or church—do you feel most challenged to offer a humble welcome? What is one way you could do that this week?

RELENTLESS GRACE
BECOMING PERSISTENT

This morning I messaged a friend to try and arrange a lunch date. We both have full schedules so it can be difficult to find time to meet, but I was confident she would accept my invitation and make time to see me because she knows I love her. And she did—we had a date sorted within minutes.

But it is not always like that. One of the mums I used to see every day at my son's preschool did not respond well to my attempts at welcome. She was cold towards me and rejected any invitations to spend time together unless we were part of a larger group. I later found out it was because she knew I was a Christian and, as an atheist, assumed we would have nothing in common.

You probably know people like that—people who just don't seem to want your welcome. Perhaps a neighbour who avoids eye contact and is always in a hurry to get somewhere when you try to talk. Or a work colleague who won't engage in conversation. Maybe a family member who expects you to make all the effort to keep in contact. Or a friend who only has time to see you when there's a problem he needs help with. Maybe you know someone like the woman I mentioned above—who doesn't want anything to do with you because of your faith.

It's easy to feel hurt or frustrated when a relationship feels one-sided or when our attempts at welcome are rejected. And it's tempting to give up—especially when we feel offended. It can seem pointless persisting with people who don't want us when others are desperate for friendship. Should we really persevere in being hospitable to people who don't respond well?

The best way to answer that question is to ask: what would God do? We find out in the story of Jonah—who was just as reluctant as we are to pursue the difficult and the undeserving. But God persisted.

A RELUCTANT PROPHET

The word of the LORD came to Jonah son of Amittai:
"Go to the great city of Nineveh and preach against it."
(Jonah 1 v 1-2)

But Jonah doesn't want to. Instead he boards a boat that will take him as far from Nineveh as possible.

It is not hard to understand why Jonah might be reluctant to obey God. Nineveh was the capital of the Assyrian Empire, known for its violence and wickedness. Jonah was likely to be harmed—or even killed—as he preached against it. That puts into perspective our experiences with people who are just distant or cold!

So Jonah runs away; but God doesn't just let him go. He pursues Jonah—the first example of persistence in this story. He sends a storm that threatens to destroy the boat. Everyone panics, afraid for their lives. But Jonah knows he is to blame. He tells the sailors to throw him overboard so that the storm will end. As the waters close over him and he sinks to the bottom of the sea, Jonah cries out to God, and God rescues him—by sending a giant fish to swallow him whole.

After three days, the fish spits Jonah onto the land. God commands him again to go to Nineveh with his message of judgment. And, this time, Jonah obeys.

"Forty more days and Nineveh will be overthrown," he proclaims in the streets of Nineveh (3 v 4). How will the violent Ninevites respond to this threat of destruction?

The Ninevites believed God. A fast was proclaimed, and all of them, from the greatest to the least, put on sackcloth. (3 v 5)

Amazingly, the Ninevites believe Jonah's message and cry out for God to have mercy on them. How will God respond? He has seen their wickedness. He's justly angry with them (v 9). Will he change his mind because the Ninevites suddenly change their behaviour? The resentful Jonah hopes not; but, of course, God does change his mind. He is merciful to the Ninevites—just as he has been to Jonah.

Perhaps, like Jonah, you struggle to understand why God would give such wicked people the opportunity to repent and receive mercy. It's particularly surprising when we learn that the Assyrian Empire would eventually invade Israel and send God's people into exile (2 Kings 17). God knew the Ninevites would fall back into their violent ways. Why persist in sending someone to warn them of judgment?

The story of Jonah teaches us that God is reluctant to give up on people. He is patient—not wanting anyone to perish, but everyone to come to repentance (2 Peter 3 v 9).

SLOW TO ANGER

Towards the end of the story, when the Ninevites turn from their violence and seek God's mercy, we discover the real reason for Jonah's reluctance to go to Nineveh.

> *Isn't this what I said, LORD, when I was still at home?*
> *That is what I tried to forestall by fleeing to Tarshish.*
> *I knew that you are a gracious and compassionate*
> *God, slow to anger and abounding in love, a God who*
> *relents from sending calamity. Now, LORD, take away*
> *my life, for it is better for me to die than to live.*
> *(Jonah 4 v 2-3)*

Jonah didn't run from God's mission because he was afraid the Ninevites would reject his message—he ran because he was afraid they would accept it! Although he had eventually obeyed God in going to them, he still secretly hoped they wouldn't repent. He wanted God to do them harm, not good.

In many ways, Jonah is the opposite of the good Samaritan, who we thought about in chapter 2. He lacks compassion for those who are not like him. He forgets that God has shown undeserved compassion and kindness to him; or perhaps he believes that he deserves God's mercy more than the Ninevites.

You and I can be like this too. Have you ever thought that someone doesn't deserve your welcome, or wondered why you should always be the one to make the effort? It's easy to think like this; but when we do, we are betraying the fact that we believe that we deserve mercy and compassion more than the people around us.

The Lord persists in pursuing those who reject him, because he is compassionate, gracious and slow to anger. His character of persistent love and faithfulness meant he was persistent with Jonah. God could easily have sent another, more obedient prophet to Nineveh but, instead, he pursued Jonah. And he was willing to go to extraordinary lengths to get him back—even using a giant fish to rescue him from death!

But this is nothing new. God has always dealt compassionately with his disobedient and rebellious people— persistently pursuing and calling them back to himself.

In the Garden of Eden, after Adam and Eve sinned, God called, "Where are you?" (Genesis 3 v 9). He was saying, *I still want to know you. You've messed up, you've been disobedient, you've rejected me—but I still love you. I want to know you, and I want you to know me. Come back to me.* It was the heartfelt plea of a rejected father calling his rebellious children home, assuring them of his loving welcome.

God continued to pursue his people as they disobeyed him and rejected his rule. He rescued the Israelites from slavery in Egypt and, despite their rebellion against him in the desert, faithfully led them to the land he had promised them. They disobeyed his law and worshipped the gods of the surrounding nations, but when they were oppressed by their enemies, he provided judges to save them. As they continued to reject his rule, he sent prophets to lead the way back to him. Eventually, they were taken into exile—but still God persisted in pursuing them. He called them to return to him and promised that, if they did…

I will heal their waywardness and love them freely, for my anger has turned away from them. (Hosea 14 v 4)

Jonah, the disobedient prophet, nevertheless foreshadows the most extraordinary person through whom God demonstrated his persistent love: the obedient Son, who was hurled into the storm of God's wrath and judgment to bring peace and safety to others. Unlike Jonah, who *nearly* died, Jesus *did* die and spent three days in the ground. He suffered the torment of being separated from his Father. But God raised him to life—just as he had raised Jonah from "deep in the realm of the dead" (Jonah 2 v 1). Jesus is the one "greater than Jonah" (Matthew 12 v 41) who not only called people back to God but brought them salvation itself.

NO GHOSTING

In our culture, "ghosting" is far more common than persistence—and it's not restricted to social media or dating apps. It has become increasingly normal for people to suddenly withdraw or disappear from long-term friendships or family relationships, either because there is conflict or tension or when they have just had enough. In a recent survey of American adults, nearly 40% said they'd been ghosted by a friend.*

But God never ghosts his friends. He doesn't withdraw or give us the silent treatment because we've irritated or offended him once too often. And he doesn't allow us to ghost him either. Jonah tried, but God pursued him—all the way to the depths of the sea. If he is willing to pursue his people with such relentless grace, we should be willing to do the same for those he has put in our lives.

If I'm honest, there are people I am half-hearted about welcoming. I am secretly relieved when they don't accept my invitations. I am reluctant to persist in offering welcome because, deep down, I'm more committed to my own comfort than to their good. I like to think that I wouldn't make the fuss that Jonah did, but really I'm not so unlike him.

It's hard to persist with people whom we find difficult or who don't seem to appreciate our efforts, but don't assume that it's pointless. Some people seem distant or unfriendly simply because they find conversation difficult or they are not used to people taking an interest in them. Others are cautious in forming new relationships because they've been hurt or betrayed in the past. Many will be used to people withdrawing rather than persevering with friendship when it's hard; it may take time for them to trust that you are genuine in your welcome. But in a culture of ghosting, persistence in hospitality is one way to be countercultural— taking people by surprise, just as God's grace does.

* www.psychologytoday.com/gb/blog/close-encounters/201803/what-do-we-know-about-ghosting (accessed on 9 Jan. 2020).

In the story of Jonah, God doesn't appear to be hospitable to the Ninevites: he sends Jonah with a message of judgment rather than an invitation of welcome. But his warning is, in fact, an expression of love. He wants the Ninevites to turn from their wickedness and be saved. The warning is necessary if they are to know his welcome.

As we persist in sharing God's invitation of welcome with our unbelieving friends and neighbours, we will also need to warn them of the consequences of rejecting him. This can feel uncomfortable and painful—especially if they react badly—but it is a loving thing to do. And our willingness to persist in offering friendship after these awkward conversations will show we are genuine.

It took a while for me to build a relationship with the woman I mentioned at the beginning of this chapter. I had to persist in inviting her to my home or to the park with our children; when she began to accept my invitations, our conversations were often awkward. I tried to learn about things she was interested in and looked for opportunities to offer help when it was needed. Over time, she learned to trust that I wouldn't preach at her or try to brainwash her children with my religious views. It was hard work, but I'm glad I persisted. A few years later, when this woman's marriage was in trouble, she turned up on my doorstep looking for comfort and help. She thought that, as a Christian, I might be more compassionate than her other friends!

My friend no longer describes herself as an atheist. She hasn't accepted Jesus as her Saviour (yet), but she says she knows that God is real because she sees how my relationship with him impacts the way I treat others.

I'm amazed because I often fail to be generous, compassionate and humble. But I'm also encouraged that, despite my failure, God reveals himself through my everyday interactions.

SHOULD WE EVER GIVE UP?
At this point we do need to ask about situations in which it *is* right to stop offering welcome to people who continue to reject us. How do we know if—or when—it may be time to stop?

It's helpful to consider first what are not good reasons to stop persisting in welcome:

- It's uncomfortable or awkward for me.
- It's too costly in terms of my time or energy.
- I'm too busy to make time for people who aren't interested in me or who hurt me.
- I fear what people may think or say about me.

None of these reasons for giving up are consistent with what the Bible teaches about how God treats us or about how we are to treat others. So is it ever ok to stop persisting?

In Matthew 10, Jesus sends his disciples to the towns and villages of Israel to proclaim that his kingdom is near. He tells them that if they are not welcomed—if their message is not accepted—they are to move on; as they leave, they are to "shake the dust off [their] feet" (Matthew 10 v 14).

Jews would have understood this action as a sign that those who had not welcomed the disciples were being viewed as Gentiles—people outside of God's kingdom. It's a warning that those who reject the message of Jesus' kingdom are rejecting God—and that if they do not repent, they will face judgment.

There may be times when it is wise to stop proactively sharing the gospel—perhaps in the face of consistent rejection. But we should persist in showing compassion when we can. God wants all people to be saved and come to a knowledge of the truth (1 Timothy 2 v 4). This should be our desire too. We know there are people who will reject God, but we don't know who he will choose to save; so we should offer welcome whenever we are able.

If you have started to build a friendship with someone, you can continue to invite them to spend time with you—in your home or elsewhere—and look for opportunities to show kindness. And, if you believe it is wise to stop pursuing a friendship, you can continue to pray for that person's salvation. Perhaps you won't do this as regularly as you used to—it would be a huge task to pray consistently for everyone you meet! But try asking the Holy Spirit to prompt you to pray for those he may be working in. I have lost contact with most of my school friends, but there are a couple who are still on my prayer list. I only pray for them every few months or if I see something that reminds me of them—but maybe God is working in them.

It's possible that you may need to distance yourself from a relationship that is physically or emotionally harmful. This is not a cold or unloving thing to do. It is right to stop affirming sinful behaviour—in the hope that God will bring those who cling to sin to repentance. In this kind of situation, you should ask for help and advice from wise and godly people whom you trust.

For the majority of us, however, the biggest challenge isn't knowing when to wisely stop pursuing people but how to faithfully persist. How can we continue to reflect God's welcome when we're not getting much back?

KEEP IN MIND...

Here are some things to remember which will help you persist in offering welcome to those who reject you.

First, remember the purpose of hospitality. You are looking to offer far more than food or friendship. The goal is always to showcase God's generous, big-hearted welcome and to offer his invitation to eternal life. As those who have received grace, we want to share it with others. So when you invite a neighbour or colleague to spend time with you and they don't accept, don't shrug it off with an "Oh well, I tried!" attitude. Remember that there is something important at stake. That will help you to want to pursue further opportunities to show friendship.

Second, remember that we are involved in a spiritual battle. If you are not alert, rejection can be used by Satan as a roadblock to keep you from pursing those whom God is calling. You may give up too easily and miss opportunities to point people to Christ. You may also miss opportunities for discipleship within the church.

Third, remember that your interactions matter. Your words and actions will either point people towards God or away from him. This means that every attempt to welcome others is significant, whether it's received well or not. Every kind word, every offer of help and every warm invitation communicates love and commitment to those you are seeking to reach. And it is a witness to those who are watching. When we persevere in reaching out to people who are rude or bad-tempered or uninterested in us, we show the difference the gospel makes in the way we view and relate to others. We prove that God's grace transforms us. It equips us to persistently pursue the graceless, even when it is costly and painful—just as it was for Jesus.

PERSISTING IN MERCY

The end of Jonah's story holds one last encouragement towards persistence.

Jonah is cross because God has been good to Nineveh. He is like an angry child throwing a tantrum when the toy he wants is given to someone else. He sits in the sun and waits for what he hopes will happen: the destruction of the city. God provides a plant to shelter him, and Jonah is content for a while; but when God sends a worm that chews up the plant, the prophet's anger is fuelled again.

Jonah is self-righteous and unreasonable, but God is patient with him. He uses the encounter to reveal more of his compassion.

But God said to Jonah, "Is it right for you to be angry about the plant?"

"It is," he said. "And I'm so angry I wish I were dead."

But the LORD said, "You have been concerned about this plant, though you did not tend it or make it grow. It sprang up overnight and died overnight. And should I not have concern for the great city of Nineveh, in which there are more than a hundred and twenty thousand people who cannot tell their right hand from their left—and also many animals?" (Jonah 4 v 9-11)

The book of Jonah ends here. God has the last word, and it is a word about his compassion for the lost—along with an implicit challenge to Jonah that he too should care more for the lost than for his own comfort. Jonah views the Ninevites as hateful enemies deserving anger and judgment. God, meanwhile, is grieved by their sin but does not delight in their judgement. He views them as helplessly and hopelessly lost without him. He pities them and, in his compassion, wants to give them the opportunity to receive mercy.

This is a word to us about how we view people who sin against us. There is no room for self-righteousness. As people whose lives have been transformed by God's compassion, we must show compassion—not contempt—towards those who offend us. We must be willing to move towards them in love. We don't need to put up a wall of self-protection against hurt or offence, because we are eternally protected by the one who took our offences on himself. We don't need to fear human rejection, because we will never be rejected by God.

My friend Tamar and her mum Jo are great examples of this. In 1997 Tamar's parents were brutally attacked as they travelled through Hungary to Romania with aid packages. Tamar's dad was killed in the attack and her mum, Jo, suffered serious injuries. In a TV interview from her hospital bed, Jo spoke about her faith in Jesus and her desire for her husband's killers to know him too. As she listened, Tamar wrestled with her own feelings of anger and hatred for the men who had killed her dad and beaten her mum. Asking God to help her to love and forgive them, she found that he transformed her emotions instantly. She too was able to forgive and to pray for the men to be saved.

Jo returned to Hungary for the trial. She visited the men, gave them care packages and Bibles, and told them she had forgiven them. She could easily have felt that she had done enough, but Jo was persistent in her desire to for them to be saved. She continued to pray for the men and asked to keep in touch with them. Istvan Dudas—the man who had beaten her husband to death—agreed, and Jo wrote regularly to him and his family for several years, sharing God's offer of forgiveness. She even went back to Hungary to visit them a couple more times, before health issues prevented her from travelling.

Years later, Istvan wrote to tell Jo and Tamar that he had asked God to forgive him and had trusted in Jesus' death for his salvation. Jo's compassion had led her to pursue her husband's killer with the offer of forgiveness and eternal life in Christ. Because of her persistent willing-ness to reach out in love, this man received life. He titled his letter, "I caused death but received life in exchange".

Tamar's story is unique; but the same extraordinary transformation is also possible in our own hearts and in the hearts of those we pursue. The right and best response to God's mercy is to persist in sharing it with others.

QUESTIONS FOR REFLECTION

How does reflecting on God's persistence—both with Jonah and with the Ninevites—encourage you to persevere with people who reject your efforts at welcome?

Think of the person you find it most difficult to persist in welcoming. What makes it difficult for you? How does this chapter help you?

How will it change your hospitality to remember that every interaction will either point someone towards God or away from him?

TAILOR-MADE

BECOMING AWARE

M y friend Paul moved to a new city a few months ago. He loves his new church—especially his small group—and enjoys serving in the music team, but it's taking a while to make friends with the other guys his age. It's not that they don't make the effort to include him; one in particular is always inviting Paul to watch the rugby with them. But, while Paul appreciates this guy's persistence, he rarely accepts the invitation because he finds large, loud groups intimidating—and he knows nothing about sport!

We saw in the last chapter that persistence is important if we are to welcome people as God does. But persistence is pointless if we're not aware of people's individual needs. One of the wonderful things about Jesus was his aware-ness of the particular needs of each person he met—and his willingness to meet them in the most helpful way.

"WILL YOU GIVE ME A DRINK?"

The woman hadn't expected to meet anyone at the well. Everyone else came to draw water in the cooler hours but, for her, the noonday heat was more bearable than the judgmental stares and whispered words of her neighbours. Some treated her with pity, but most condemned her for her string of failed relationships.

Jesus was different. He saw her in a way that others didn't. He had initiated a conversation—even though he was a Jew and she a Samaritan. He was patient and gentle with her, but he was also unafraid to confront her sin. Rather than avoid the awkward subject of her living arrangements, he addressed it head on.

He told her, "Go, call your husband and come back."

"I have no husband," she replied.

Jesus said to her, "You are right when you say you have no husband. The fact is, you have had five husbands, and the man you now have is not your husband."

(John 4 v 16-18)

Jesus knew why this woman had come to the well in the middle of the day. He was aware of her sinful circumstances and her sense of shame. He knew what she needed: not another man who would ruin her life but one who would give her life.

He wanted her to know that he was the only one who could truly satisfy her.

"I MUST STAY AT YOUR HOUSE"

Zacchaeus was not popular in Jericho. As a chief tax collector for the Romans, he was despised by the local community. He had made himself rich by cheating people out of their money—adding a little extra here and there to the taxes he collected. He had chosen wealth over social acceptance and was facing the consequences. He was an outcast.

Zacchaeus wanted to see Jesus as he passed through the town. But the crowd lining the streets was large, and Zacchaeus was small. He ran ahead of the crowd and climbed into the branches of a sycamore tree where he would have the perfect view. Nestled in the tree's branches, he should have been inconspicuous; but Jesus stopped right below and called for him to come down. Jesus didn't confront Zacchaeus about his dishonesty and greed. He just invited himself round to Zacchaeus' home. Zacchaeus climbed down as quickly as he could to welcome him.

Both Zacchaeus and the woman at the well needed acceptance, grace and forgiveness—but Jesus dealt with each of them differently. Their unique situations and their individual fears and desires shaped his interactions with them.

The Samaritan woman had been publicly disgraced by her failed relationships and was ashamed of her own sin. She needed Jesus' gentle rebuke, but she also needed his acceptance and offer of new life. Zacchaeus was just as sinful. He loved money more than he loved God, and he regularly sinned against his neighbours by cheating them out of their income. He, too, needed to know that he could be forgiven and accepted by Jesus. And, because he had sinned against his neighbours, he needed the opportunity to publicly repent and make amends. For these two very different individuals, the end result was the same: they were accepted by Jesus and welcomed into his kingdom.

After their encounters with Jesus, both began to interact differently with others. Jesus' acceptance of Zacchaeus changed his heart so that he was no longer greedy but generous.

> *Look, Lord! Here and now I give half of my possessions to the poor, and if I have cheated anybody out of anything, I will pay back four times the amount. (Luke 19 v 8)*

And, after Jesus' gentle confrontation, the Samaritan woman no longer feared meeting her neighbours but ran back to her town to tell them everything.

> *Come, see a man who told me everything I've ever done.*
> *(John 4 v 29)*

Many of the Samaritans from the town believed in Jesus when they heard the woman's story and met him themselves. Like Zacchaeus, she was no longer an object of shame but an instrument of grace.

"PLEASE COME!"
Jairus had heard about Jesus. All the synagogue leaders were aware of his teaching—and most of them disapproved.

But Jesus healed people, and Jairus was desperate: his only daughter was dying. Falling at Jesus' feet, he begged him to come to his house.

The woman followed cautiously at first, trying not to draw any attention to herself. An outcast for twelve years, this woman was suffering from a chronic illness that had stripped her of her dignity. The constant bleeding made her—and everything she touched—unclean. She couldn't worship at the temple. She couldn't even touch another human. But she *would* touch the edge of Jesus' cloak.

Then joy and fear mingled as the woman felt her bleeding stop and heard Jesus' voice.

Who touched my clothes? (Mark 5 v 30)

Trembling, she fell at his feet and—in front of the watching crowd—told him everything.

She needn't have feared. Jesus was tender with her. He had healed her, and now he affirmed her publicly:

Daughter, your faith has healed you. Go in peace and be freed from your suffering. (v 34)

Jairus had been watching impatiently as Jesus delayed healing his daughter to focus on this woman. Jesus was still speaking to her when messengers arrived from Jairus' house to tell him that it was too late—his daughter had already died.

Don't be afraid; just believe. (v 36)

Jesus took Jairus into the house where his daughter lay. Taking her hand, he spoke gently:

Little girl, I say to you, get up! (v 41)

Jairus, his daughter, and the woman in the crowd needed to experience Jesus' power, but Jesus met their needs differently. He could have healed the woman and Jairus' daughter at the same time—he had healed from a distance before (Luke 7 v 1-10). But while he responded immediately to the woman's need, he delayed going with Jairus.

Rather than letting the woman escape unnoticed, he gave her the opportunity to be seen and heard. He made sure everyone would know that she was clean—and that he had commended her faith. But Jairus was already respected in his community and didn't need public affirmation. What he needed was greater faith in Jesus. Jairus had asked for a healing miracle, but Jesus wanted to give him more.

Jesus did what was best for each of them, showing both his extraordinary power over death and his concern for very ordinary needs. The woman was healed; Jairus was "completely astonished" (v 42). As for the little girl, she was raised to life and began to walk around—and Jesus even took the time to tell her parents to give her something to eat.

TAILOR-MADE HOSPITALITY

For Jesus, welcome was personal. He didn't adopt a "one size fits all" approach. He treated everyone he met as an individual—with specific needs and desires. He responded in unique ways to the unique people he encountered. As we seek to reflect him in his welcome, we can do the same.

You and I can't be all-knowing as Jesus was, but we can work at discerning what may be most helpful and appreciated by those we are seeking to welcome. This takes time, effort and wisdom on our part. We need to resist the temptation to be formulaic in our efforts at hospitality. One size doesn't fit all—our welcome must be made to measure.

The kind of superficial hospitality portrayed on social media or TV shows is often impersonal because its focus is on the host rather than the guest. It's all about the quality of the cooking, the artistry of the presentation or the wittiness of the conversation. It's a way of showing off. We are like this too when we become more concerned with meeting our own needs than the needs of others. Our focus may be impressing others or putting a tick next to the "hospitality" box on our list of spiritual disciplines. We may be looking to what we can get out of hospitality—affirmation, respect, fun or friendship—rather than what we can give.

Jesus-shaped hospitality is personal and others-focused. He cared about everyday practical needs such as food and rest. He cared about suffering, pain, grief, loneliness and shame.

I have compassion for these people ... I do not want to send them away hungry. (Matthew 15 v 32)

Do you want to get well? (John 5 v 6)

Come with me by yourselves to a quiet place and get some rest. (Mark 6 v 31)

What do you want me to do for you? (Mark 10 v 51)

Sometimes Jesus showed he was aware of a need by meeting it before he was asked. On other occasions he allowed people to express their desires to him before he acted. He knew that the blind man wanted to see and that the disabled man wanted to walk, but he gave each of them permission to express what they wanted. This is something we don't always think of doing—we often prefer to second-guess what someone wants. But Jesus didn't hesitate to ask questions. It was a way of showing that he cared for individuals.

I am not Jesus (obviously!), but I suffer with a Messiah complex at times. I think I know exactly what someone needs from me or exactly what they need to do to improve their circumstances. I am less willing to take the time to listen well to an expressed desire or to pray for discernment and wisdom before assuming I know best. I need to learn from Jesus. I need to become aware.

GROWING IN AWARENESS

When you invite someone to spend time with you, try to think about what will make them feel most welcomed and valued. You could even ask them directly: what helps in their specific circumstances? Don't assume it will be the same as for the last person you invited. Think about what it looks like to make space in your life for them in particular.

My friend Rachel has no family of her own but appreciates being welcomed into the day-to-day life of a family from her church. She enjoys sharing regular meals with them, joining them for holidays, and being able to pop round whenever she likes. But although she is grateful for this welcome, Rachel still doesn't feel completely part of the family—because they don't share their struggles with her or ask things of her that only family would. She wants them to take advantage of her a bit: to ask big favours, to share their heartaches and to impose on her for help when they know it may not be convenient. That's what would make her feel as though she really belongs.

This family are genuine in their desire to welcome Rachel into their lives—and, in many ways, they are a good example of how we should care for one another within the church family. But they aren't completely aware of what Rachel needs. If the giving is all one-way, she will always feel like a project rather than a true family member. She longs to feel needed rather than needy.

When Rachel told me this, it challenged me. It made me think again about some of the assumptions I have made in the past—especially about my single friends. I have assumed that they want me to look after them, provide for them and offer a safe place for them in my home. I haven't stopped to consider that they may, at times, want to look after me, provide for me, offer a safe place for me. Even as I have tried to be welcoming, I have focused more on what I want to offer to them rather than on what they want from me.

It is also easy to make wrong assumptions about what would be most helpful for people who are finding life tough because of illness or some other kind of suffering. For example, I remember an occasion when my husband and I invited a woman who was going through a difficult time to join us for dinner. I pulled out all the stops to prepare a beautiful meal that I thought would show comfort and care for this woman. But as the conversation inevitably turned towards her circumstances, she pushed her food half-heartedly round the plate—fighting her lack of appetite so she wouldn't appear ungrateful. Although we assured her it was fine to leave the meal uneaten, we could sense her discomfort.

I realise now that, while my intentions were good, I had focused more on what I wanted to do for this woman than on what she really needed from me. A simple mug of tea and a box of tissues would have been far more appropriate!

So what will it look like to be more aware in the way we offer welcome? To show hospitality that is others-focused rather than self-focused?

It may seem daunting at first. But focusing on individual needs, rather than a "How to be a good host" checklist, can actually be liberating. If you've ever been put off offering hospitality because you don't think you can "do it properly", be encouraged! You don't need to follow a script. You don't need to copy others. And you don't need to exhaust yourself learning new skills.

I have intentionally tried to avoid being overly prescriptive in this book. Your circumstances are different to mine, and the people we seek to welcome will also be different. But here are three suggestions to help you become more aware in your hospitality.

Pay attention

Next time you're at a church gathering, look around and try to identify some of the particular needs of your church family. Last Sunday, I made a list of a few different needs I had become aware of so I could think and pray about who I could reach out to and how to best do that. (I'm sure I missed loads, but it gave me a starting point.) In particular, I made a note of...

- new people
- people going through especially difficult trials
- those suffering bereavement, loneliness, anxiety, or depression
- single friends

I haven't had the time (or emotional capacity) to connect with everyone on my list—it will probably take me a number of weeks to do that. But it has helped me pray more thoughtfully and think more carefully about what may be appreciated by different people. Some I have just messaged to tell them I have noticed them and am praying for them. I've found opportunities to sit with others in a Bible study, include them on a night out, drop a small gift round to their house, or arrange to meet up with them later in the month (and these things haven't taken much time). One single friend loves to cook but has complicated living arrangements, so I've invited her to bring a meal round to share with my husband and me at our home next Tuesday. She's looking forward to an evening out, and I'm looking forward to a night off from cooking!

We can try to do the same with our neighbours and work colleagues. It's unlikely we'll be able to make time for all of them every week, but as we pay attention more, we will understand people better and become more aware of specific needs or desires. We can then pray and look for opportunities to show people that we see them and care about them.

It is helpful to remember that this aspect of hospitality doesn't rely on your own circumstances being easy or comfortable. Even if you are struggling yourself, it is still possible to focus on being aware of others' needs. For example, when my friend Hazel was in hospital being treated for throat cancer, she was very attentive to the needs of those around her—making opportunities to encourage the nurses on her ward and offer comfort to the other patients and their families, even though it was painful for her to speak.

If you love to cook but can't invite people to your home, why not look out for stressed mums for whom you could provide meals occasionally? You could even invite yourself to eat with them so you can help with the children. If you're lonely, try to notice others who sit on their own or don't seem to have lots of friends, and invite them to watch a film with you. If, like my friend Rachel, you feel you're always the one imposing on a particular friend or family, try to find ways of serving them without being asked. Our own struggles and challenges don't have to stop us from paying attention to the needs of those around us.

Be flexible
Life in our Western culture often feels pressured and frenzied. It's easy for the calendar to become so full that

we have no time (or energy) left to embrace unexpected opportunities to show welcome. Many of us leave little or no margin so that we can spontaneously invite a lonely work colleague home for a meal or call someone who has been missing from church for a couple of weeks.

Sometimes the busyness is unavoidable because of pressing deadlines, extra meetings or unexpected crises. But sometimes it's a result of choices we have made—to pursue promotion, to excel academically, to enrol our children in lots of extra-curricular activities. Whatever the reasons, a full schedule can hinder hospitality. Would it be possible for you to keep some time in the schedule that isn't accounted for? If you do, you can then be available for a friend or neighbour who needs encouragement, or engage in longer conversations with colleagues, or offer practical help to someone in need, without feeling overly stressed or under pressure. Hospitality flourishes when we are able to be flexible with our time and our plans.

Yesterday evening, just as I was trying to finish this chapter, a friend arrived for dinner—an hour and a half early! I am ashamed to admit that underneath my welcoming embrace was a grumpy and grudging heart. "How inconsiderate! Doesn't she realise I have work to do? When will I get to do the things I've planned?" These thoughts whirled around my mind for a good part of the evening— sapping my joy and hindering my welcome. I had to fight to reorient my focus from my own desire for space to my friend's need for company and encouragement.

Hospitality involves a willingness to adjust our plans to suit specific needs. That may be as simple as being willing to drive across town to meet someone at their place of work rather than at your home; or sitting somewhere different at church next Sunday. Or it may mean the inconvenience of last-minute food shopping or preparation for an unexpected guest who has special dietary requirements. Our willingness to be flexible—both in *how* we show hospitality and in *when* we show it—will help us as we become more aware of individual needs.

Keep trying!

Despite our best efforts to be thoughtful and sensitive, we will sometimes get it wrong. We all sometimes misread people or misunderstand their circumstances. And what someone needs or wants can change from one day to the next. But the discouragement of not getting it quite right shouldn't cause us to retreat. If you've tried to show welcome in a particular way and it hasn't worked, try something else. Ask others to help you discern what may be more appropriate. Or ask the person themselves what they would find helpful—most people will appreciate any effort we make to show welcome and care towards them. More importantly, God sees our hearts and delights to see us seeking to be like him in our welcome.

Perhaps you feel your circumstances make it impossible for you to think about others' needs: you have so many of your own. When we feel like this, Jesus' example is challenging. Even at the worst moment of his life, he continued to be aware of others. As he suffered on the cross, his mind was not focused only on his own pain. Looking at his grieving mother and his close friend, John, he said:

Here is your son ... Here is your mother.
(John 19 v 26-27)

He saw their needs and provided for them. John would take Mary into his home and care for her as if she were his own mother. Mary would love John as if he were her own son.

Jesus was just as aware of his loved ones' immediate, practical needs as he was of their eternal, spiritual needs—and on the cross he provided for both. Growing in awareness means growing more like him.

QUESTIONS FOR REFLECTION

How did Jesus' awareness of an individual's specific needs impact the way he interacted with them?

How are you tempted to use a "one size fits all" method of hospitality? How can you adopt a "made to measure" approach?

Think of someone—perhaps in your church family or at work—who would be encouraged by a welcome that is tailor-made. How can you show hospitality to them in a way that best meets their specific needs?

OVERTURNING TABLES

BECOMING INCLUSIVE

Having arrived in town a bit early, Mez McConnell—
an inner-city pastor who dresses in a hoodie and
beanie—decided to pop into the church building where
he was due to speak later that day. When he got there, he
was greeted by some women who asked for his voucher.*

Mez was a little confused. "I don't have a voucher," he
replied. "I'm just here to look around."

The women said that wouldn't be possible—and
called some men over to help enforce the voucher rule.
After a while, it became clear that the vouchers were
for a food bank run by members of the church. Dressed
in his usual street style, Mez had been mistaken for a
homeless person in need of food. And he wasn't getting
any without a voucher!

---

* That's a coupon if you're in the US. Mez told this story in a talk at an Acts
29 conference, *The Gospel and Class*, in September 2018 (www.youtube.com/
watch?v=tcVrSIOF9Kk).

Needless to say, it shouldn't be like this. God's welcome in Christ is inclusive: regardless of what you look like, where you come from or how you speak, you are welcome. And this is something which he invites us to reflect in our own welcome.

So far this book has focused mainly on our hospitality as individuals. In this chapter, we're going to consider our corporate welcome as God's people. It is time to think about how our church communities can become places of greater welcome—especially for those who are often excluded elsewhere.

CLEARING TABLES

Mark's Gospel records a shocking incident that took place in the temple courts during the last week of Jesus' life.

Jesus enters Jerusalem with his disciples and makes his way to the temple. In the outermost court, the Court of the Gentiles, crowds of travellers press against the tables of the money-changers, impatient to exchange their foreign money for coins that can be used in the temple. Others haggle noisily with the merchants selling lambs, doves, pigeons, salt and wine for the Passover sacrifices. Jesus observes the temple-turned-market scene with rising sorrow and righteous anger. You probably already know what happens next:

Jesus entered the temple courts and began driving out those who were buying and selling there. He overturned the tables of the money-changers and the benches of those selling doves, and would not allow anyone to carry merchandise through the temple courts.

*And as he taught them, he said, "Is it not written:
'My house will be called a house of prayer for all
nations'? But you have made it 'a den of robbers'."*
(Mark 11 v 15-17)

The Court of the Gentiles is the place where everyone—
Jews and non-Jews—could pray and worship. The Jews
should be using that area to call everyone to *Come*. Instead
they fill it with trade, which should take place outside the
temple courts, preventing Gentiles from praying. The
temple is no longer a house of prayer for all nations.

This bustling bazaar is also getting in the way of Jewish
visitors. Instead of being welcomed into a place of prayer,
where they can bring their requests to God, they are
met with people who want their money. They can't go in
without a voucher! The money-changing may seem like
something inclusive—enabling Jews from far away to
change their foreign currency and join in the temple sacrifices. But it is excluding them from the one thing that is
really important about coming to the temple: prayer.

Jesus quotes from Isaiah 56, where God had explicitly stated his intention to gather the nations into his
kingdom. Although they were invited to pray in the
temple (1 Kings 8 v 41-43), non-Israelites were excluded
from participating in sacrifices offered on the temple
altar. But Isaiah's prophecy looked ahead to a time when
their offerings would be acceptable to God.

*And foreigners who bind themselves to the LORD
    to minister to him,
to love the name of the LORD,*

and to be his servants ...
these I will bring to my holy mountain
  and give them joy in my house of prayer.
Their burnt offerings and sacrifices
  will be accepted on my altar;
for my house will be called
  a house of prayer for all nations. (Isaiah 56 v 6-7)

Jesus was restoring the temple to what it should have been: a place of prayer for all people. But he was also the one who would fulfil Isaiah's words and bring far deeper inclusivity than the Court of the Gentiles could ever provide, even once the market had been cleared away and the court was back to its proper function. Through his death and resurrection Jesus would make a way for all people—Jew and Gentile, rich and poor, old and young—to come to God *together*. To worship him *together*. To experience his presence and joy *together*.

As we wait for the ultimate fulfilment of this glorious vision, we can mirror it in our church families. And we must. Jesus' anger towards those who were hindering "outsiders" from inclusion in temple worship is a warning for us as we consider our attitude to welcome in the church. Being inclusive is not an optional extra.

BARRIERS OF OUR OWN
The places where we gather as a church family are our "Courts of the Gentiles". This is where we should offer inclusive welcome. But, like the Jewish leaders, we often fail. We put up our own money-changing tables. We might not explicitly state restrictions about who can

join us, but it's likely that there are some obstacles to worship for those we should be calling to come.

If you're not sure what I mean by this, think about the following scenarios.

Kai is new to the area and tries out the nearest church. He introduces himself to a group of people at the coffee bar and they are friendly, but it's clear from the conversation that they have all known each other for years. Soon he has no idea what they are talking about—and nobody stops to explain all the in-jokes. It feels like a club he could never belong to.

Leyla grew up in a church but left when her parents divorced. She has spent the last ten years looking for acceptance in all the wrong places, and wonders whether she should try church again. She looks through the websites of some local churches. "Everyone looks so polished and perfect," she thinks. "They could never welcome a mess like me."

Mike spent most of his twenties and thirties in and out of rehab. He's been clean for 15 years now and has recently come to know Jesus. His friend Zaid has been taking him to church. He likes the songs and people are friendly, but the pastor often preaches about the evils of alcohol and drugs, and every time he does, Mike feels condemned. Zaid has told him that all his sin has been forgiven, but he's starting to wonder if there really is grace enough for him.

My fourth scenario is a personal experience of exclusion in church. A few years ago, I visited a large city church with a friend. I was already feeling a bit out of place in my scruffy jeans when everyone suddenly stood to sing a hymn

I'd never heard before. I quickly grabbed a hymn book and began frantically flicking through the pages, trying to find the words so I could join in. But the hymn wasn't there. Everyone knew the words by heart! I felt totally out of place—as though I'd crashed a party I wasn't invited to.

Could any of those situations happen in your church? It's easier than we might think to unintentionally make people feel unwelcome or excluded.

INCLUSIVELY EXCLUSIVE

As we think about inclusiveness, we need to acknowledge what seems to be a paradox within the gospel message. Critics of the gospel argue that insisting there is only one way to be saved is not at all inclusive—rather it is exclusive. In a society that is obsessed with tolerance, that is abhorrently intolerant. But is that true? Is the gospel exclusive or inclusive?

Jesus said:

> *I am the way and the truth and the life. No one comes to the Father except through me. (John 14 v 6)*

> *Small is the gate and narrow the road that leads to life. (Matthew 7 v 14)*

The apostle Peter declared:

> *Salvation is found in no one else, for there is no other name under heaven given to mankind by which we must be saved. (Acts 4 v 12)*

There is only one way to be saved. That is an exclusive claim. But it's inclusively exclusive. Anyone can be saved by that one way. The path that leads to life is a narrow path—but anyone can follow it. Only Jesus can save—but he will save anyone who calls on him.

This is the beautiful message of the gospel. Jesus offers salvation to anyone—regardless of their culture, class, gender, occupation, religion, sexuality or sin. So, even as we insist that there is only one way to be saved, we must offer that way with arms open wide. The exclusiveness of the gospel gives us even more reason to be inclusive. It adds urgency as we share the good news of God's welcome.

REMOVING THE BARRIERS

So what will it look like to reflect God's image in our welcome of the outsider? What are the tables we may need to overthrow in order to make space for those who might otherwise be excluded? I want to suggest four potential barriers that could hinder people from feeling comfortable, accepted and valued in our churches.

Race

In Revelation 7, John records a stunning vision that should excite and motivate us in our welcome:

> *After this I looked, and there before me was a great multitude that no one could count, from every nation, tribe, people and language, standing before the throne and before the Lamb. They were wearing white robes and were holding palm branches in their hands. And they cried out in a loud voice:*

"Salvation belongs to our God,
who sits on the throne,
and to the Lamb." (Revelation 7 v 9-10)

This is the goal of welcome: a diverse people, gathered around the throne, worshipping the Lamb with one voice.

It's easy to shake our heads at the Jewish leaders' failure in the Court of the Gentiles but be blind to our own. I know people who would never consider themselves racist but, in practice, they only spend time with people who look like them, and they withdraw from opportunities to share the traditions and experiences of people from other cultures. But this isn't how we reflect God in his welcome. Rather, we should delight to show off our unity by proactively looking for ways to welcome and include people from all cultures—in our corporate worship gatherings as well as our homes.

One specific way we can show off our delight in diversity is in our response to refugees and immigrants. While neighbours or work colleagues may react with fear-driven hostility, Christians will want to respond with faith-fuelled hospitality. We will want to welcome our brothers and sisters from other countries—many of whom are fleeing persecution—with love and generosity. We will want to welcome those from other religious backgrounds with compassion and grace, in hopeful anticipation that our hospitality will display the beauty of the gospel and reflect the glory of the God we know.

My church has a ministry among Japanese women in our city. Some women from the church run a weekly English conversation class where they seek to build friendships with these women, most of whom can't speak English well. A few of them also meet every two weeks to look at a Bible passage together.

Every few months our women's Bible-study group invites the Japanese language class to come and help us understand more about Japanese culture. We share food, try on kimonos, attempt origami projects and enjoy chatting to one another. Last Christmas, we introduced our Japanese friends to some English Christmas traditions, including mince pies and Christingles, while they taught us how to sing *Silent Night* in Japanese! Our aim is simple: we want to show our Japanese friends that we value them and want them to be part of our church family.

Who are the people groups God is bringing into your neighbourhood—your street, your local shops, your workplace, your children's school? How will you seek to welcome them into your church community?

Poverty

> *"People don't want to be projects. The poor need a welcome to replace their marginalisation, inclusion to replace their exclusion, a place where they matter to replace their powerlessness. They need community. They need the Christian community."*
>
> *(Tim Chester, A Meal with Jesus, p 88)*

In chapter 1 we saw God's intention that there would be no poverty among his people when they entered the land he promised to give them (Deuteronomy 15 v 1-11): the Israelites were to be generous and open-handed to those who were in need. But God's desire was not only that the poor were provided for *by* his people; he wanted them to be fully included *among* his people. That's why he made provision for the poor in the sacrificial system: those who couldn't afford a lamb could sacrifice two small pigeons (Leviticus 14 v 21).

If God is concerned to include the poor among his people, we should be too. Helping with food banks or other forms of charity is excellent, but for Christians it is not enough. We must invite the poorest and most vulnerable people in our communities to become part of God's family.

Jesus' kingdom is "good news for the poor" (Luke 4 v 18). In one sense, this verse applies to all of us because we are all *spiritually* poor and in need of salvation. But we should also take Jesus' words literally; his kingdom is good news for the *financially* poor, the excluded and the powerless. Those who are often overlooked, taken advantage of or mistreated can be sure that Jesus will welcome them into his kingdom and treat them with dignity and honour.

As his followers, we must share this good news with those in our communities who are most needy and vulnerable. We don't want to exclude anyone. This means not just having a welcoming attitude but also taking steps to consider what barriers there may be to such people and how to remove them.

For example, if you are involved in youth activities and camps, what could you do to minimise the cost? Perhaps those who are able to could subsidise others who would struggle with payment. In my church, several women pay extra towards our women's weekend away to cover the cost of those who can't afford to pay.

You could research local charities or services you can point people to if they need help in specific areas—and make others in your church aware of these too. You could think about whether the language used in your church's services or small groups is helpful to those who have less formal education. And it is also worth considering whether the way people dress at those gatherings communicates something about who "fits" and who might not. Becoming a Christian doesn't mean adopting a particular culture or class, but we can give that impression all too easily.

Pray for your church family to be a place where those who are marginalised in society find genuine welcome and honour. And think: what can you do to make that happen?

Sexuality and gender

Most of us know people who struggle with their sexuality or gender identity in some way. Some struggle openly; others hide their suffering because of fear or shame. We may know others who intentionally embrace a transgender identity. Whether these issues are celebrated or lamented, each person will know a measure of pain. It may be centred around something they have experienced in the past, or a fear for the future. It may be a sense of rejection or isolation from those who don't understand the way they feel or the choices they have made.

These individuals may feel excluded not only from their families, friendship groups or local communities but from the church family too.

Earlier in Isaiah 56, God addresses some members of the Israelite community who felt similarly excluded.

Eunuchs were court officials who were castrated in order to make them more reliable servants of the king. The reasoning was that because they could have no family of their own, they were more likely to be loyal and trustworthy. In Israel, those who were mutilated in this way were excluded from full participation in temple worship (Deuteronomy 23 v 1; Leviticus 21 v 16-21). So as well as being unable to participate in normal family life, the eunuch was excluded from another important aspect of community life. There would inevitably have been a sense of pain and loss in this exclusion. But God offers the hope of inclusion. He promises to welcome such people.

> *"To the eunuchs who keep my Sabbaths,*
> *who choose what pleases me*
> *and hold fast to my covenant—*
> *to them I will give within my temple and its walls*
> *a memorial and a name*
> *better than sons and daughters;*
> *I will give them an everlasting name*
> *that will endure for ever." (Isaiah 56 v 4-5)*

Eunuchs might never produce children of their own but, if they are part of God's eternal kingdom, their name will never disappear. If they commit themselves to the Lord, they will never be cut off from his people—they are guaranteed an inheritance that will last. They will no longer be excluded from worship but fully included in God's family.*

Issues of sexuality and gender are complicated, and

---

* If you have questions about why eunuchs were excluded from temple worship, you may find this online article by John Piper helpful: www.desiringgod.org/interviews/does-the-old-testament-alienate-the-disabled

different in many ways from the experience of the eunuchs God is speaking to in these verses. But perhaps there is a point of connection with the eunuch's experience—and fear of—exclusion. Those whose sexual attractions or experiences make it impossible for them to marry or have children of their own may wonder if they can feel fully included in a community that appears to be full of happy families. Those who feel shame because of their present struggles or past experiences may fear they could never be truly accepted—either by God or by Christians who don't appear to struggle with the same issues.

But it is possible for each one to know the loving welcome of a perfect Father and the promise of honour, relationship and a permanent place in his forever family. While we must hold fast to the Bible's teaching about sexuality and be clear about its implications for followers of Jesus, we are also called to offer God's welcome to everyone—regardless of identity or sexuality. We want those who are broken—whether by their own sin or by sin against them—to know forgiveness, healing and restoration through the gospel.

So rather than avoiding those whose experiences we don't understand, we must lovingly pursue relationships with them. We must listen carefully to their stories, ask questions and seek to understand the specific hurts or struggles they face.

Ultimately we will want to tell those who have been rejected, hurt or abused about the Father who would never hurt them but sacrificed his own Son to offer them life and freedom, a restored identity and the certain hope of a future with no pain, struggle or confusion.

Physical disability

Secular culture celebrates the strong, fit and healthy. Those who are physically weaker are often overlooked. But Jesus' kingdom is different—and that should be obvious in our churches.

In Matthew's account of the incident in the temple, courts, we find out that after Jesus had expelled the buyers and sellers, the blind and lame came to him in the temple and he healed them (Matthew 21 v 14). This was significant because the Jewish authorities had added a law to prevent anyone who was crippled, lame or blind from entering the temple. So it wasn't only the Gentiles who were excluded from temple worship—the Jewish leaders had no time for those who were sick or physically vulnerable. But Jesus did.

Our church has a growing ministry among the deaf community in our area. We include BSL (British Sign Language) interpretation in our morning services and run a weekly BSL Bible study—employing a part-time deaf community worker to make this possible. When we plan evangelistic events, we try to think about the best way to include our deaf friends. If there's a gospel talk, we make sure there's an interpreter available. When we show video clips in our services, they are subtitled.

We go one step further at Christmas: our carol services include a BSL reading by some deaf friends—interpreted into spoken English for those of us who are sign-language impaired! Having members of the deaf community reading makes the service not only accessible but truly inclusive. We are also communicating to other guests that we value everyone—just as Jesus does.

Not every church can afford to employ a deaf community worker. Not every church will be in an area with a large immigrant population. Every context is different and will need different solutions for including the excluded. But for all churches, the principle is the same. We seek to remove every unnecessary or unhelpful obstacle that could prevent people in our communities finding a welcome and a home within the family of God.

Why not invite some friends or church leaders to pray with you for specific people in your community who may struggle to feel welcome in your church? Ask God to show you, together, what obstacles may be getting in the way of welcome—and how you can remove them.

IT STARTS WITH YOU

Church families are made up of individuals, so a church will only be as inclusive as its members. If you want to be part of an inclusive community, you need to be committed to showing inclusive welcome every day of the week—not just on Sundays.

Pray that God will give you a desire to welcome those in your community who are most often excluded. Confess favouritism—where you have overlooked or failed to welcome people who are unlike you. Pray for a willingness to embrace discomfort, if necessary, so that others may feel more comfortable. And believe that God will answer!

One Monday last year, I prayed that God would help me develop more culturally diverse friendships within my neighbourhood. On the Wednesday, I noticed two Afro-Caribbean sisters moving into the house across the road. I ran straight over to welcome them and, when their kitchen flooded later that day, I was ready to help. In practice, that meant introducing them to another neighbour who is far more practical than I am! The next day I took over some flowers and (nervously) asked if they'd like to come to church with me sometime. They were there the next Sunday and have been coming regularly since.

We often limit our hospitality to people who are just like us. But Jesus calls us to something greater:

> *When you give a banquet, invite the poor, the crippled, the lame, the blind, and you will be blessed. Although they cannot repay you, you will be repaid at the resurrection of the righteous. (Luke 14 v 13-14)*

Who will you invite?

QUESTIONS FOR REFLECTION

Reflect on the ways in which God welcomes those on the margins of society. What surprises you? What encourages you?

Who are the people or people groups who may feel excluded or unwelcome in your church? What one thing could you do this Sunday to make your church more welcoming?

Think about your friendship groups. Who could you seek to include who may be overlooked or excluded in other circles? How will you seek to welcome them?

GIVEN FOR YOU

BECOMING SACRIFICIAL

We started this book with an invitation: "*Come,* all you who are thirsty".

In Isaiah 55, God invites the thirsty to come and drink from his unending supply of water. He invites those who are poor to eat and drink until they are satisfied—at no cost. He promises to provide for those who cannot provide for themselves. He offers a cheerful, big-hearted, open-handed, ungrudging, freely given, forever-satisfying welcome to all who will come.

But this isn't a takeaway meal. God invites us to a banquet—a future feast that we will eat together with all his people. In an earlier part of Isaiah's prophecy we read:

On this mountain the LORD Almighty will prepare
a feast of rich food for all peoples,

a banquet of aged wine—
the best of meats and the finest of wines.

(Isaiah 25 v 6)

Isaiah prophesies about a future day when God will gather his people to his holy mountain (his home) and welcome them. He will prepare a rich banquet for them to enjoy. And they will finally live in peace—with him and with each other. Shame will be removed, and death will be destroyed—for ever.

On this mountain he will destroy
  the shroud that enfolds all peoples,
the sheet that covers all nations;
  he will swallow up death for ever.
The Sovereign LORD will wipe away the tears
  from all faces;
he will remove his people's disgrace
  from all the earth. (v 7-8)

But for this feast to take place—for death to be destroyed—a sacrifice was needed. We saw in chapter 1 that generosity is costly. This is the reality: there can be no generosity without sacrifice.

HOSTING HURTS
In the 1987 film *Babette's Feast*, Babette is a penniless Frenchwoman who turns up on the doorstep of a small Christian community on the coast of Denmark and becomes housekeeper to two spinster sisters. For fourteen years she prepares their plain food and observes the

increasingly fragile and fractured relationships in their community. What nobody realises is that she was once the head chef at a famous café in Paris.

One day, Babette finds out that she has won the lottery of 10,000 francs back in France. But instead of using the money to return to Paris and her former lifestyle, she decides to spend it on a gourmet French dinner for the sisters and their community. The legalistic villagers, fearful that it would be a sin to enjoy such luxury, agree to eat the meal out of respect for Babette, but resolve to take no pleasure in it. They will not even talk about what they are eating. But as the meal progresses, their taste buds are awakened, and they learn to delight in the food—and in each other. Joy is rekindled, feuds are forgiven and relationships are restored. The evening ends with the renewed community holding hands and singing together under the stars.

The sisters assume that Babette will return to Paris and are shocked when she tells them she cannot go back because she has spent all her money on the feast. Babette has sacrificed all she has—including her hopes of restoration—for the benefit of her employers and the community they love. For Babette, this feast has been a last supper of sorts.

The Gospels tell the story of another last supper: the meal Jesus ate with his disciples just before he was betrayed and arrested. Have you ever noticed that as Jesus prepared to eat this meal, he anticipated the future, eternal feast? He told them:

I have eagerly desired to eat this Passover with you before I suffer. For I tell you, I will not eat it again until it finds fulfilment in the kingdom of God ... I will not drink again from the fruit of the vine until the kingdom of God comes. (Luke 22 v 15-18)

Jesus was eager to eat this meal with his disciples because he knew that his earthly life and ministry were ending. He knew he would not eat the Passover again until he was physically and permanently reunited with them—and with all his followers—at the great future feast. He was looking forward with joy to the consummation of his kingdom.

Jesus was the host of this Passover meal; he had taken care of all the arrangements for it. Earlier in the day, he had sent Peter and John into the city to meet the owner of the house they were now in. They found that Jesus had already booked the room and organised for it to be set up ready for them. He had prepared the place for his disciples to eat with him. He would now prepare a place for them in his Father's house: an eternal home where they would live with him for ever. He would secure their place at the Father's feast.

And of course Jesus did this through sacrifice. The cross towers as the highest expression of welcome in all of history. It is the means by which we are welcomed into God's new community. And it is our example as we seek to welcome others.

Over the last six chapters, we have looked at characteristics of God's welcome that we are invited to imitate in order to offer hospitality that reflects his. Each one is counterintuitive for us. Each one is costly. Each requires a measure of sacrifice. Perhaps that has put you off at times. Perhaps the invitation to share this kind of hospitality seems more like a pressure than a privilege—more duty than delight.

In this final chapter, I want to show you that the daily sacrifices we make on behalf of those we seek to welcome are real and necessary, but also to persuade you that they are totally eclipsed by the brilliance of the reward we will enjoy—both here and in eternity. As we respond to Jesus' call to be his co-hosts, following his example of sacrificial hospitality, we can be confident that we are also his guests and will one day sit with him at his table, where tears will be no more and death will have been swallowed up for ever.

LIFE, THROUGH DEATH

Before Jesus claimed his kingdom, he had to suffer. This last supper was a traditional Passover meal—an opportunity for Jews to remember their rescue from slavery in Egypt, through the death of a lamb. But this supper also pointed forward to the following day, when Jesus would give his life to rescue his people from slavery and death. Before Jesus sat at the table again, he would offer himself as a sacrifice—a Passover lamb—so that his friends might sit at the table with him.

And he took bread, gave thanks and broke it, and gave it to them, saying, "This is my body given for you; do this in remembrance of me."

In the same way, after the supper he took the cup, saying, "This cup is the new covenant in my blood, which is poured out for you." (Luke 22 v 19-20)

Like the first Passover, this meal was a symbol of rescue through sacrifice and death. The bread represented Jesus' body, which would soon be broken on the cross. The wine represented his blood, which he would shed in order to establish a new covenant with his people.

The cross was where the greatest hospitality ever known was offered, as the Son of God gave his life so that we could be welcome at his table for ever. This is why Jesus describes himself as the living bread and invites us to feast on him (John 6 v 51-55). It is an invitation to believe that this death—this broken body and shed blood—can satisfy God's righteous anger at our sin. It is an invitation to trust in Jesus' death to give us life. We feast on him now so that we may feast *with* him for eternity.

We have already seen that reflecting God's welcome means rethinking how we use our time, money, energy and skills—focusing on serving others instead of ourselves. Perhaps you feel overwhelmed by the cost of welcoming people the way God does. I hope not: I want to encourage you to see the privilege of reflecting God in your hospitality rather than make you feel guilty about what you can't do. But as we consider these characteristics of God, we inevitably recognise our failure to love as he loves and welcome as he welcomes. We realise how costly and painful hospitality can be.

Last Friday my Afro-Caribbean neighbours moved out. (It's good news—they feel so settled in the neighbourhood, and especially at church, that they have decided to put down roots and buy a house around the corner.) On Saturday the new neighbours moved in. But this time I didn't run straight over to welcome them. I know I should have been excited about the opportunity to offer generous welcome, but I was tired. The thought of starting again with new people was overwhelming. "I struggle to keep up with the people I already know," I thought. "I don't have space in my life for anyone else. What if they're needy? What if they're rude? I just want to eat my curry and watch my film."

(I did eventually make it over later that evening, and they're lovely!)

The defining hallmark of the kingdom is life. But, paradoxically, this life comes through death. Jesus was crowned as King not on a golden throne but on a wooden cross. And for his followers, the way to life is also through death. Even the small everyday sacrifices you and I make to welcome others can feel like death. They are painful. Yet they are also the way to life.

When we choose to be generous and open-handed, rather than grudging or tight-fisted, we risk the loss of temporary things; but we gain eternal treasure. When we sacrifice comfort and convenience in order to show compassion to the hurting or vulnerable, we get to experience God's grace sustaining us in new ways. As we risk our reputation or the approval of our friends by humbly welcoming and serving those who are rejected by others, we learn to find our identity in God. We depend more fully on him. We know greater joy as we choose to please him rather than people. We are aware of his Spirit sustaining and equipping us. We deepen our relationships with members of our church family who are also making sacrifices to welcome others.

Of course, we are not the only ones who are rewarded. Our sacrifices can also be life-giving for others as we provide practical care for the needy, comfort the lonely, encourage the weary, seek the lost, and support those who feel overwhelmed. This is what Paul meant when he wrote to the Corinthian Christians, "Death is at work in us, but life is at work in you" (2 Corinthians 4 v 12).

Last Christmas, a couple I know invited an older widowed man from their church to spend Christmas Day with them and their young daughter. This man is in the early stages of dementia and can be argumentative and demanding. But Chris and Pia welcomed him into their home and worked hard to make the day special for him. It wasn't easy. They prepared Christmas dinner the way he liked it, played the games that he wanted to play (and let him win!), and watched the television programmes he insisted on watching rather than their usual family film. He didn't have any Christmas presents apart from the ones they had bought him, so their daughter waited until evening and opened her gifts after he had gone so that he wouldn't feel left out. It was a big, genuine sacrifice for their family. But it had a huge impact on this man, who would otherwise have been lonely and sad.

Persisting in pursuing those who reject our welcome, working hard at understanding how to meet different needs and trying to include those who are often excluded can be physically tiring and emotionally draining. It is sometimes frustrating, often uncomfortable, always costly. But the rewards are worth it.

RULES AND REWARDS

Just after Jesus tells his disciples that one of them will betray him, the conversation takes a surprising turn.

The disciples begin to argue about which of them would be considered the greatest. Every time I read this chapter I'm struck by the disciples' pride. Jesus has just told them that he will be betrayed and killed—and they respond by arguing over status! But I'm also struck by Jesus' gracious response. He reminds the disciples of the rules of the kingdom, but also of their reward.

> *The greatest among you should be like the youngest, and the one who rules like the one who serves. For who is greater, the one who is at the table or the one who serves? Is it not the one who is at the table? But I am among you as one who serves. You are those who have stood by me in my trials. And I confer on you a kingdom, just as my Father conferred one on me, so that you may eat and drink at my table in my kingdom and sit on thrones, judging the twelve tribes of Israel. (Luke 22 v 26-30)*

Jesus' kingdom does not operate by the rules of this world—because Jesus doesn't. He is the supreme ruler of the kingdom, but, as we saw in chapter 3, he comes down from his position of greatness in order to serve. He is comfortable with humility. Most of us, meanwhile, are more like the disciples—self-centred rather than others-focused. Our goal is more often personal pleasure than sacrificial service.

Perhaps, like me, you can think of times when you have refused to sacrifice your time or energy to offer hospitality to someone in need. You've chosen a quiet evening in front of the television rather than making a phone call or arranging to see a friend, neighbour or colleague who is suffering in some way. Sometimes, that's the right choice—our bodies do need rest, and our minds need to switch off. But often it is a self-centred choice: a choice to worship self rather than to serve another. I rarely feel satisfied or refreshed when I make that choice with that motivation. Rather, I feel unproductive and dissatisfied.

But when, out of love for Jesus and a desire to serve others, I put myself out to make the phone call or open my home, I am encouraged. Even if the conversation is hard work or emotionally draining, I am satisfied that I have pleased my King and reflected his grace in some small way.

Let me underline that this will look different for all of us. Consider your own capacity and remember the importance of rest (which God also commands us to do). You need to be honest with yourself about what you can and can't do. If you struggle with chronic fatigue, for example, or have infant twins, or work two jobs to make ends meet, then you may end up comparing yourself unfavourably with others: "I can't make the kind of sacrifices that person can make." But we are not all called to make the same sacrifices as one another. The point is to be willing to make sacrifices where you can—while making sure that you have time to rest, to worship and to be served yourself.

The priorities of Jesus' kingdom conflict with the priorities of this world. In his kingdom, greatness is not defined by status but by service; not by ability but by attitude. Jesus reminded his disciples not to look to the world but to him. He had just served them by washing their feet. Soon he would serve them by giving his life.

Jesus invites his followers to serve alongside him. But he also promises that, one day, they will rule alongside him. He is the King of the kingdom, but he will share his rule with those who have shared in his suffering. They will sit with him at the future feast.

This is a promise to you and me. As we sacrifice our time, energy, resources and comfort in order to welcome others, we can be confident that Jesus will reward us abundantly.

A NEW LIFE

At the end of *Babette's Feast*, we learn that Babette did not view her last supper simply as a way of expressing gratitude to the sisters for taking her in. When she tells them that she has spent her last franc on the feast, one of them exclaims, "Babette, you ought not to have given away all you had for our sake." But Babette replies, "It wasn't just for your sake."

In her hurried escape from danger fourteen years earlier, Babette never fully mourned the sorrows that brought her to this community—the brutal murder of her husband and son, and the loss of her home, lifestyle and reputation as a celebrated chef. But as she plans, prepares and serves her feast, Babette relives and puts to rest the grief of her past. She closes the door to her old life—and, with it, the opportunity to return. She chooses to embrace her new life and fully commit herself to her new community.

As followers of Jesus, we have the opportunity to do the same. We can close the door on our old life and fully embrace our new life in Christ. Through his sacrifice, Jesus has given us a new identity and a new community. Like Babette, we have found a place where we can belong—eternally. Our hospitality towards one another is a way in which we live out our identity as new people, committed to each other. And our hospitality towards those who are not yet Christians is motivated by our desire to see them join this forever family. We embrace sacrificial hospitality because we want to see the lives of our friends, neighbours and colleagues transformed too.

I have had the joy of witnessing this kind of transformation in my friend Sofia. Before she became a Christian, Sofia rarely left home. An abusive relationship had left her with no self-worth, and she suffered with extreme anxiety. But when Jana introduced her to Jesus, she felt overwhelmed by his sacrifice for her and was desperate to know him better. She started going to church and was quickly made to feel welcome. She found that people were genuinely interested in her. They listened to her, invited her into their homes and offered practical help and support. Her life was completely transformed. She is now full of joy and loves to share her story with others who don't yet know Christ. Like Babette, she has fully embraced her new identity and her new community.

EXTRAORDINARY IN THE ORDINARY

In 1732, two young German men—Johann Leonhard Dober and David Nitschmann—felt called to go to an island in the Dutch West Indies to share the gospel with over 2,000 African slaves who would otherwise never hear of Jesus. They were told it would be impossible to reach these slaves with the gospel because their owner, an atheist, refused to let a preacher near them. But Dober and Nitschmann were so determined to share the gospel with these slaves that they said they would be willing to sell themselves into slavery alongside them in order to do so.

It's unclear whether the men were actually sold as slaves or whether they managed to live as free men among the Africans. But what is clear is their willingness to sacrifice their freedom so that some of these slaves might become part of God's family—that they might be welcomed at the Father's feast.

These men were extraordinary. I feel very ordinary in comparison. You probably do too. But we can be encouraged that our ordinary lives—and our very ordinary acts of hospitality—may also result in more people being gathered at the feast.

Sacrificial hospitality is hard—it's much easier to write about than it is to practise. But there is great joy in knowing we are engaging in work that is purposeful and fruitful. As I write, I'm thinking about members of my church family who are struggling to persevere in their faith. If my hospitality can encourage them to resist temptation, pursue holiness and grow in faith and love, then I will sacrifice my time and energy joyfully. I'm also thinking about my neighbours and friends who do not know Christ. If my hospitality can showcase his welcome and point them towards life, the joy I will experience in seeing them at the future feast surpasses any sacrifice I may make on their behalf.

Welcome is costly. It involves sacrifice. But it is also glorious. We get to follow the example of our Saviour—laying down our own lives so that others may live (Luke 9 v 24; Philippians 2 v 17). We get to hold out God's offer of life to those who don't know him (Matthew 28 v 19).

We get to share his words of life with those who are weary, discouraged, battling sin and in need of comfort, assurance and hope.

Jonathan Edwards, the eighteenth-century theologian, prayed, "Lord, stamp eternity on my eyeballs". As we consider the sacrifices involved in offering welcome to others—and are maybe overwhelmed by those sacrifices—we can pray, "Lord, stamp on my eyeballs a vision of the future feast! Help me joyfully anticipate my place at that feast—and the brothers and sisters who will be there with me. Use my hospitality to lead others there." And as we pray this, we can be praying with faith that, although we may feel insignificant or insecure, God can use our ordinary hospitality to achieve extraordinary things.

QUESTIONS FOR REFLECTION

Think of someone you would like to show welcome to. In what ways could your sacrificial hospitality be life-giving for that person?

How can your hospitality show that you have new life and a new identity in Christ? How is God calling you to embrace this new life more in the way you welcome others—both within and outside the church family?

How will Isaiah's vision of the future feast encourage and motivate you to persevere in showing hospitality even when it feels costly and painful?

AFTERWORD

In 2020, during the coronavirus pandemic, my church family worshipped in front of our screens, in separate homes. We prayed and studied together via Zoom, Skype and phone. From the first week of the lockdown, I desperately longed for the day when we would be together again. The longer we were apart, the more we looked forward to being reunited.

At that time, the superficial images of hospitality our culture portrays became completely irrelevant. But these seven characteristics of welcome that we see in our God were—and always are—unchanging. Being generous, compassionate, humble, persistent, aware, inclusive and sacrificial was just as possible in lockdown as it always has been, even though that looked a bit different to usual.

And as we emerge from that period of anxiety and suffering, the great hope of a place at God's eternal feast is now even more enticing. I long for the day when God will swallow up death, wipe the tears from every face and tell us to sit with him—for ever.

In that day they will say,

"Surely this is our God;
we trusted in him, and he saved us.
This is the LORD, we trusted in him;
let us rejoice and be glad in his salvation."
(Isaiah 25 v 9)

As we look forward to that day, let's join him in offering welcome in every way we can. Let's seek to become generous, compassionate, humble, persistent, aware, inclusive—and ready to sacrifice whatever we have for the sake of the One who sacrificed all.

THANK YOU...

Christopher Ash, for generously writing the foreword. Everyone at The Good Book Company who worked on this book. I am especially grateful to Katy Morgan. Your diligence, wisdom and thoughtful insights have encouraged me throughout the process. Thank you for being excited about the message and for improving my communication of it.

Matt Searles, for reading parts of the manuscript and giving feedback. And for being an enthusiastic champion of this book.

Friends, whose stories I have shared.

Tiana and Jed, for your cheerful support and encouragement. It is a joy to watch you becoming more like Jesus and growing in your love for his church. I pray you will reflect his welcome throughout your lives.

Richard, for reading the first drafts and still believing in this project! Thank you for always pushing me to use my gifts and encouraging me to persevere. It is a privilege to journey through this life with you.

And to my Saviour, who loved and welcomed me first. It is my greatest honour to declare his praises.

the good book
COMPANY

BIBLICAL | RELEVANT | ACCESSIBLE

At The Good Book Company, we are dedicated to helping Christians and local churches grow. We believe that God's growth process always starts with hearing clearly what he has said to us through his timeless word—the Bible.

Ever since we opened our doors in 1991, we have been striving to produce Bible-based resources that bring glory to God. We have grown to become an international provider of user-friendly resources to the Christian community, with believers of all backgrounds and denominations using our books, Bible studies, devotionals, evangelistic resources, and DVD-based courses.

We want to equip ordinary Christians to live for Christ day by day, and churches to grow in their knowledge of God, their love for one another, and the effectiveness of their outreach.

Call us for a discussion of your needs or visit one of our local websites for more information on the resources and services we provide.

Your friends at The Good Book Company

thegoodbook.com | thegoodbook.co.uk
thegoodbook.com.au | thegoodbook.co.nz
thegoodbook.co.in